Ethical Business Relationships:
Partnerships in Peace

Ethical
Business
Relationships

Partnerships in Peace

Lee B. Thomas, Jr.

BUTLER BOOKS

Dedicated to my wife, Dr. Joan Thomas.
She paid a big price in supporting me as
I traveled the globe in search of business
and peace. She was at home with three
children and practicing medicine in the
poverty areas of Louisville. We've had a
great 57 years together.

ISBN 1-884532-69-1

Printed in Canada by Friesens Printers

For information address Butler Books
P.O.Box 7311, Louisville, KY 40207
502-897-9393
billbutler@insightbb.com
www.butlerbooks.com

Acknowledgments

At Vermont American Corp., and now at Universal Woods, I have taken the cue from my mentors and tried to run our business operations ethically. My mentors in ethical business dealings were my parents, Lee B. Thomas Sr. and Margaret L. Thomas; Wight Bakke, my counselor at Yale and a fellow Quaker; and Jackson Smart, managing partner at the CPA firm of Touche Ross Bailey & Smart. My mentors today are our son Glenn, who owns and operates Chromatography Research Supplies Inc. in Louisville, Kentucky, and Paul Neumann, who runs our company here in Louisville – Universal Woods. You'll be reading about all of them in great depth in this book.

I am also indebted to a lot of people for helping to put this book together. To cite just a few of them: Ron Cooper helped edit out the misspellings and grammatical errors. Jan Arnow worked with the publisher to organize the book for general readers. And my old friends from Vermont American remembered and wrote some wonderful flashbacks.

Contents

Foreword

Throughout the business world, Lee B. Thomas, Jr. is known as an outstanding executive, earning this reputation through his work as president and CEO, then chairman, of Vermont American Corporation and for the past 12 years as chairman of Universal Woods, Inc. Around the Bellarmine University W. Fielding Rubel School of Business, however, Lee is also known for his outstanding contributions to student learning as an instructor in his role as Executive-in-Residence.

Lee has authored a very important book that examines many important subjects relevant to successfully managing a business enterprise in today's complex, difficult environment. To encourage careful thought, Lee has included specific, critical examples from his career to clearly highlight the importance of doing business the "right way". Lee emphasizes that business decisions raise important social, financial and moral questions for each of us and society as a whole. Lee makes a persuasive argument that businesses play a critical role in shaping the global landscape and correctly concludes that economic decisions mold our characters, affect the quality of individuals' lives or can cause frustration and despair. Critical subjects discussed in the book include:

- The important role the world business community should play in improving economic and social conditions.

- How "human dignity" refers to the sacredness or value of each person as an end, not simply as a means to the fulfillment of the bottom line of a business.

- Business behavior can affect relationships among nations and the prosperity and well being of us all. Business is often the first contact between nations and, by the way in which it causes social and economic changes, has a significant impact on the level of fear or confidence felt by people worldwide.

- How a business must maintain its own economic health and viability, but that survival is not a sufficient goal. Businesses have a role to play in improving the lives of all their customers and employees.

- How businesses, as responsible citizens of the local, national, regional and global communities in which they operate, play a critical part in shaping the future of those communities.

On the first day of all finance classes, I explain the primary goal of any financial manager is to make decisions that will maximize shareholder value. It is very important for readers to understand that this goal is entirely consistent with the role of management outlined by Lee in this book. Firms that do not act in an ethical manner and make decisions that do not further the public good will incur costs that probably will exceed the benefits of those decisions. As shown over and over the past few years, unethical decisions by firms and individuals will result in declining sales, negative publicity and legal action – all which lead to costs that come directly out of shareholder wealth. These costs will be avoided by readers who pay close attention to Lee's thoughts outlined in the book.

Whether Lee's in the board room, the classroom or the in this book, Lee always conveys the finest characteristics of leadership and ethics.

I have team-taught many times with Lee and he has set a standard for ethical decision-making that is very easy to follow: "The Mother Test": If you are thinking of doing something you can't tell your mother about – don't do it! Enjoy Lee's book.

— *Daniel L. Bauer, DBA*
Dean, W. Fielding Rubel School of Business
Bellarmine University
Louisville, Kentucky

Introduction

Well, my friends, I guess there's some business I just plain don't need.

About 1960, Leo Weill, owner of Leo's Hideaway seafood restaurant on Jefferson Street in Louisville, Kentucky, was reported to have made that statement at his restaurant. I'm told a black couple came in and without any fanfare Leo seated them. This upset a table of white folks. They got up and, using all kinds of bad language, stormed out of the restaurant. Leo went to the door, turned around, faced his patrons and proclaimed, "Well, my friends, I guess there's some business I just plain don't need."

And so we had the first integrated restaurant in Louisville. Simple as that. When my wife Joan and I went to eat at Leo's afterward, we found Abraham Lincoln's Emancipation Proclamation on everyone's table. It was inspirational to me to have a guy with the courage to stand up in public for something he believed in.

During nearly 70 years in business, from the time I sold magazines as a kid, I've tried to stand up for what I believe in. Whether it was refusing to do business with a Chinese factory that had deplorable working conditions, or asking a manufacturer of army tanks to get another source. I've spent a lot of time figuring out what God's will is for me. I'm convinced there are a whole lot of people out there that want to do the right thing once it becomes possible. Making it possible is what leadership and ethical business is all about.

Satygraha, or soul force, is what Mahatma Gandhi

preached in his lifelong pursuit of peace. I've tried to bring the force of the soul to controversial situations to avoid violence. And I've often said, like my friend Leo, "Well, my friends, I guess there's some business I just plain don't need."

This book is about my mentors, the lessons they taught me, and the lessons they are still teaching me today. It's about ethical principles in business, something instilled in me by my parents and many others. It's about translating those principles into ethical behavior in the workplace. It's about how we always should be striving to be honest and honorable in our dealings. It's about how we need to form peaceful partnerships so that everyone comes out a winner. It's about ethical values driving the way we manage business. And finally, it's about trying to discern God's will for us as we face the often-difficult challenges of doing business today.

The Enron, Arthur Andersen and other debacles in business dealings of late have forced us to face this ugly fact: some American companies have not acted ethically. They have given business a black eye, and we must do better.

Many say the whole purpose of being in business is to enrich your stockholders. That's it. There is no other purpose. But I believe that value-based decision making, coupled with intelligence, is the best way to run a successful business. I have always believed that we have an obligation to all of our stakeholders. This means all of the parties with whom we do business and the communities where we are located.

At Johnson & Johnson, they have no mission statement. Instead, for more than 60 years, a simple, one-page document – "Our Credo" – has guided their actions in fulfilling their responsibilities to their customers, employees, and their stockholders. The last sentence of that credo states, "When we operate according to these principles, the stockholders should realize a fair return."

Moral integrity and ethics pays. You can do well by doing good.

Chapter 1 **Character**

Ethics was a Thomas family tradition. That point was driven home to me when, of all places, I was sitting bare naked in a Jacuzzi. This occurred at a fat farm in Tucson, Arizona a couple of years ago. Another guy was sitting there, too, just as naked as I was. We struck up a conversation and I learned he had worked for a lighting fixture business. It turns out that company was Thomas Industries, a business that my dad started. What a coincidence!

When I introduced myself as Lee Thomas Jr., he said, "Let me tell you something. Your dad's handshake was better than any contract ever written. When your dad died, the ethics of the company deteriorated, so I quit." I told him that I was on the Thomas board when Dad died, and I quit for the same reason. (Thomas Industries did eventually get its ethical act together, as we discuss later in the book).

My grandfather, Rees Thomas, was a hardware merchant in Sumas, Washington, near the Canadian border. From a very early age my dad worked in his store. Dad became a tinsmith, a necessary occupation for a hardware man. When you're doing business with your friends and neighbors, you have to be ethical – otherwise, you don't have any business.

My mother's father, Gomer Thomas, was Rees's brother. He was a small-town attorney in Bellingham, Washington.

Backstory: Thomas Industries

In 1948, Lee B. Thomas, Sr. acquired a residential lighting fixture company, with a group of investors, from the Moe family of Fort Atkinson, Wisconsin. The company's name was changed in 1949 from Moe Brothers to Moe Light, Inc. Their lighting fixture production swelled in 1952 when the company purchased Star Lighting Fixture Company of Los Angeles, and opened a residential lighting factory in Princeton, Kentucky. The following year marked the beginning of the company's real growth when Moe Light, Inc. was merged into the Electric Sprayit Company of Sheboygan, Wisconsin, a paint sprayer manufacturer, and the name was changed to Thomas Industries Inc. In 1955, Thomas Industries' stock was first offered to the public and the company moved its headquarters to Louisville, Kentucky, to more efficiently manage its expanding group of products. In the late fifties, the Benjamin Electric Company and C&M Products of Canada were acquired by Thomas Industries, positioning Thomas as a leading manufacturer of a full range of lighting – commercial, industrial and residential. On October 4, 1967, Thomas Industries' stock began trading on the New York Stock Exchange. Throughout the sixties and seventies, Thomas continued to diversify its product lines, acquiring companies that manufactured paint brushes and rollers, specialty tools for the commercial construction industry, grandfather and decorative wall clocks, fireplace screens and accessories, metal chimneys and zero clearance fireplaces, wallpaper, artificial and preserved floral arrangements, table lamps, barbeque grills and built-in vacuum systems. Most recently, Thomas Industries was sold to Gardner Denver on July 1, 2005.

He wasn't one of those litigious guys you find so often in today's legal world. He never went to college. He got into the profession the hard way: by reading the law and taking the bar exam. He was thoroughly ethical. He was also chairman of the local school board.

My mother was a professor at the University of Washington at a time when it was very unusual for a woman to be in that kind of position. She had her master's degree in chemistry, and taught mathematics and, if memory serves me well, chemistry. When I got into trouble with my studies, she was a big help. (More about Mother later in the book.)

So you would have to say that an ethical character was ingrained in me from an early age. I learned many lessons from my early mentors.

Lesson One: Destroying free enterprise

At the age of nine years old, I was selling *Ladies Home Journal, Liberty* and *Saturday Evening Post* door-to-door in the small Illinois town where I grew up. One day I had leftover copies, so I took them to the train station to peddle.

A big kid hung out there selling his own magazines, and he was convinced the train station was his territory. He beat the heck out of me and took my money. (I wish I could say it was Bill Gates I tangled with, but he wasn't born yet.) What happened is a real good lesson on how to destroy the free enterprise system. We've got to have open competition if we're going to have the right kind of system that will benefit the most people. And I learned that lesson very young.

Lesson Two: Not all churches are moral

I was 10- or 11-years-old when I had a job setting pins in a bowling alley. This was before the days of automatic pinsetters, and those darn balls would come roaring down the alley and those pins would fly everywhere. Once in a while, a pin would fly out of the pit. Can you imagine children being subjected to that kind of danger? It was pure idiocy. And this was not a private-sector outfit. This was in the basement of the church – and the church was taking the profits!

Lesson Three: Questionable caddies

During the Depression most of the caddies at local golf courses were adults. These caddies were also operating a brothel and a bootleg liquor business on the edge of the golf course. We lived in a dry town. Of course, their little enterprise was as illegal as it could be. I kept my mouth shut and didn't tell anybody. Today's misbehavior by chief executives is nothing new. We had it back when I was a kid, too.

Lesson Four: The end doesn't justify the means

My contemporaries and I competed to land one of several jobs as lifeguards on Lake Michigan. We took the Red Cross life-saving test for a time, and a written test. I studied hard. I had no trouble with the written test. But, regrettably, I stacked the deck in my favor for the swimming test. There were two fellows who wanted the fun of working with me. So anytime we needed to "save" someone, I would pick them. That way we'd have two people kicking instead of one! It was much faster that way, and our competition couldn't keep up. The end result was that I won the swimming test and got the job. I was a good lifeguard and was conscientious about it. But it wasn't kosher. I don't think that I did the right thing by doing the wrong thing and keeping my mouth shut about it.

Lesson Five: The truth sometimes hurts

When I was 15-years-old, the local police officer, Mr. Bentley, saw me take away the right-of-way from an elderly woman in the rain while I was driving, and he pulled me over. "Lee, I'm not going to give you a ticket. Instead, you go home and tell your daddy what you did and you have him call me." Of course, I'd rather have had the ticket.

Lesson Six: Lessons in parents' marriage

One of the things I learned really early is that you need to try to accomplish good things – with or without the law. My parents taught me this at a very early age. My parents' marriage would have been illegal in the state of Washington because they were first cousins. So they eloped to Canada and got married up there. When they returned, because of reciprocity, their marriage was recognized in the States. They accomplished a good thing by a sort of circuitous route.

My parents were great mentors. For her time, Mother was a "mild feminist," if I can call her that. Her maiden name, Margaret L. Thomas, is on her tombstone and on a scholarship fund at the Community Foundation of Louisville. She and I talked a great deal about human relationships, and her advice was very good indeed. (Many of our conversations took place at the Jewish Standard Country Club in Louisville, where she would eat Yiddish food because it reminded her of her mother's German cooking.)

Backstory: The Community Foundation of Louisville

The first philanthropic trust for the Louisville, Kentucky community was created in 1916 as the Louisville Foundation, and was reorganized in 1984 as The Community Foundation of Louisville (CFL). From 1984 until the present, CFL grew from three charitable funds and assets of $1.4 million to more than 1,000 funds totaling nearly $200 million. Although commingled as a lasting community resource, each fund has its own name and charitable purpose as defined by its donors. In 2004, CFL funds awarded $23 million in grants and distributions to nonprofit organizations, and many scholarships to individuals that improve the quality of life in the Louisville area and beyond.

Chapter 2 **Peace**

My dad did an ingenious thing: he encouraged me to quit high school and go to Yale a term early. Yale was an all-male university at that time. Since it was wartime and most young men were already serving in the military, they badly needed students. So they just looked in your ear – if they didn't see light, you got admitted. Because I had matriculated at Yale before I was drafted, they had to take me when I came back after the war – and I wasn't that good of a student. I could never have gotten into Yale had I applied after the war without having been previously admitted. At that point, both returning service men and high school graduates were trying to get in college. It was much more competitive.

Pretty darn smart, my father

However, I wasn't ready to go to college and I did very poorly. I flunked freshman English cold. I was on probation when I was drafted into the Army.

I began working at a desk job and didn't realize how good I had it. Then I had a run-in with a sergeant and told him off in no uncertain terms. It was a costly mistake. I was transferred to another company and found myself in the company of misfits. Perhaps one-third of them were parolees. It was a rag-tag bunch and we were at the bottom of the rung in the military caste system.

After fighting across Mindanao in the Philippines, we made the amphibious landing at Sarangani Bay. In war, it's unbelievable how quickly you lose your values. As a soldier, I was taught that the Japanese were animals. We were forced to watch all those hate films that depicted Japanese as being sub-human. It was all part of the indoctrination process. We were killing them, and I was pulling the trigger along with everybody else.

My company was being trained to become the first wave of the invasion of Japan. I figured that certain death awaited my comrades and me.

Lloyd Berg, an editor for the Fellowship of Reconciliation, captured the mood well in his article about my wartime experiences, "The Man Who Rejoiced in the Bomb." (*FOR Witness*, 1995):

> *They were also being trained to be the first wave of any invasion – essentially, to die on the beaches after distracting the enemy enough so that subsequent waves could run over their bodies and have a chance.*
>
> *As all this registered, it became clear in Thomas' mind that he would never see home again. He was there to die, he was going to die, and that was all there was to it.*
>
> *Such thoughts permeated the hold of a landing craft, with Thomas aboard, as it sailed north through the Pacific. The men felt certain they were headed for their last moments of life, leading an invasion of Japan.*
>
> *A loudspeaker announcement suddenly shattered the gloom. It seemed the best news that could have been dreamed of, prayed for, or imagined. A great new*

weapon! One bomb to wipe out a city! This would end the war! He would live, after all! Return home! Have a good life!

If this news was not quite akin to Resurrection, it would have seemed to do until the real thing comes along. Life and hope were almost miraculously being given back to Thomas, it seemed.

I saw Hiroshima shortly after it was bombed. It was an experience that would change my life forever. Despite the headline in the *FOR Witness* article, I didn't rejoice in what I saw. This was a city where the destruction was simply beyond description. It was colossal. I was only there for a few hours, but the memories have lasted a lifetime. When we got to the occupation camp, we put out our garbage cans and the Japanese dove in and ate raw garbage. They were starving. They weren't the sub-humans that our Army films showed. They were ordinary people. Like us, they carried pictures of their loved ones, some of whom had been killed in the war. They were grieving, just like we were. I was deeply moved.

After the war in the Pacific ended, we started to do something right: employing the local people to help us and to help them get back on their feet. Because of my business background, the Army put me in the excellent position of being in charge of the payroll for the Japanese who were working on the base. It's awfully easy to make friends when you're passing out checks and so I became friends with some of these great people. Later I would return to Japan in much happier times. (See "Poking Fun in Japan" in Chapter 12.)

My time in Japan set the moral tone for the rest of my

life and set me on a path to try to act fairly and ethically in all of my dealings. I came home with two overriding concerns: world peace and race relations.

Back at Yale

During World War II, my mother was sending back all of the letters that I had written with the grammar corrected. I thanked her for doing that because I drastically needed to improve my English skills. While I was in foxholes, I also wrote English papers for a guy who was in another company. He had been in the English department of a college back home. In a war you're not always fighting. One of your big problems is boredom, waiting around for the battle to resume. I took advantage of the frequent lulls to work on my writing and grammar. When I returned to Yale, I was ready for the English professor and I did all right.

At Yale I was lucky enough to have Wight Bakke as my counselor. Wight was clerk of the Quaker meeting at New Haven, Connecticut, a professor, my advisor for four years, and foremost expert in the world on labor relations. (The latter would prove fortuitous for me later on.) He got me interested in the Religious Society of Friends (Quakers), a group dedicated to peaceful conflict resolution and cooperation. What a mentor Wight turned out to be!

While in college, because of my interest in labor relations, I went to a Quaker work camp run by the American Friends Service Committee in a working class section of Philadelphia. The idea was to get a job in a union plant – mine was at a bubble gum factory. We joined the union and went to union meetings. And in the evening we got some instruction on labor relations from both the company and union sides.

Backstory: E. Wight Bakke (1929-1971)

E. Wight Bakke was born in Onawa, Iowa, to Harriet Frances (Wight) and Oscar Christian Bakke, a shoe merchant in Onawa. Bakke attended Northwestern University where he received a BA in Philosophy in 1926. He continued in the Yale Divinity School from 1926 to 1929. His graduate study in social sciences was also conducted at Yale University, and from 1931-1932 he was the Sterling Fellow at Yale, receiving his Ph.D. in 1932. In 1964 he received an honorary LL.D. from Northwestern University.

Bakke taught sociology at Yale from 1932-1934, and was an assistant professor of economics from 1934-1938. He served the Institute of Human Relations as Director of Unemployment Studies from 1934-1939, and was promoted to Professor of Economics in 1938 and appointed the Sterling Professor of Economics in 1940. Bakke was the Director of Graduate Studies in Economics at Yale from 1940-1950.

From 1944 until the late 1950s he directed Yale's Labor and Management Center. The Center was devised with a nine-member policy committee made up of three representatives of Yale, three from labor, and three from management to develop a balanced approach and avoid an "ivory tower" view of labor relations.

Bakke was often called upon to advise governmental commissions and scholarly organizations on labor and management issues. He was Fulbright professor in Denmark in 1953, the principal consulting social economist for the Social Security Board from 1936-1939, and a consultant to the Department of Labor, Navy Department. He directed the National Bureau of Economic Research, and was the Chairman of the Appeals Committee of the National War Labor Board. He was a member of several Presidential Emergency Boards and the National Manpower Policy Task Force.

All this came at a time of frequent violence on the picket line. I had seen enough violence in the war. We learned something about trying to achieve cooperation and partnerships. It was a heck of an experience and it helped set me on a sure-footed spiritual path.

Soon after, I became a Quaker.

Quakerism was founded in England by George Fox (1624-1691), a non-conformist religious reformer. At the age of 19, he left home on a four-year spiritual search, eventually feeling a direct call from God to become an itinerant preacher and promote the concept of the "inward light," or "inner voice" – a belief that an element of God's spirit exists within every person's soul, allowing everyone to comprehend the Word of God and to express opinions on spiritual matters.

Fox taught his followers to worship in silence. At their meetings, people would speak only when they felt moved by the Holy Spirit. They thought of themselves as friends of Jesus and referred to themselves as "Friends of Truth" (from John 15:15). Later, they became known simply as "Friends."

The movement came into conflict both with Cromwell's Puritan government and later with the restored monarchy of Charles II, over a number of points: they refused to pay tithes to the state Church; to take oaths in court; to practice "hat honor" (doff their hats to the king or other persons in positions of power); or to engage in combat during wartime. They developed an intense concern for the disadvantaged, including slaves, prisoners and inmates of asylums. They agitated for an end to slavery, and for improvements in living conditions in penitentiaries and treatments in mental institutions.

Fox was persecuted during his lifetime and frequently imprisoned. During one such time, he suggested that the judge "tremble at the word of the Lord." The judge sarcastically referred to Fox as a quaker; the term stuck, and has become the popular name for the Religious Society of Friends.

As in England the first Quakers to arrive in America were viewed as dangerous heretics. They were deported as witches, imprisoned or hung, but many found a sanctuary in the Rhode Island colony, which had been founded on the principle of religious tolerance. William Penn (1644-1718) and other Quakers played a major role in the creation of the colonies of West Jersey (1675) and Pennsylvania (1682), colonies that were noted for their toleration of minority religious groups.

Following the Revolutionary War, a number of Quaker organizations were formed to promote social change in the areas of slavery, prison conditions, poverty, Native American affairs, etc. Quakers played a major role in organizing and running the Underground Railroad aiding runaway slaves' escape to freedom in the northern states and Canada.

The first and second World Wars created a crisis for the Quaker movement. Until that time, the Religious Society of Friends was a pacifist organization. During the two wars, however, some men were excited by the nationalistic fervor, and entered the armed forces. Throughout World War II, many American Quakers joined the Friends Ambulance Unit, an unofficial body supported by British Quakers, which allowed Quakers to volunteer as medical and ambulance personnel on the battlefields.

Today, there are about 300,000 members worldwide. As with all large faith traditions, individual Quakers are religiously diverse, but the following beliefs are common to most Quakers:

Friends believe that there exists element of God's spirit in every human soul. Thus all persons have inherent worth, independent of their gender, race, age, nationality, religion, and sexual orientation.

Quakers' opposition to sexism, racism, religious intolerance, warfare and the death penalty comes from this belief.

Simplicity, pacifism, and inner revelation are also long-standing Quaker beliefs.

Their religion does not consist of accepting specific beliefs or of engaging in certain practices; it involves each person's direct experience of God.

Many do not regard the Bible as the only source of belief and conduct. They rely upon their Inner Light to resolve what they perceive as the Bible's many contradictions. They also feel free to take advantage of scientific and philosophical findings from other sources.

All aspects of life are sacramental; they do not differentiate between the secular and the religious. No one day or one place or one activity is any more spiritual than any other.

No defense-related work, thank you

Quakers do not believe in fighting in a war, and do not participate in the preparation for war. For me, at Vermont American, that meant canceling a pretty good-sized contract with the U.S. Defense Department.

Before I would accept a job with my dad at Vermont American, I had one major condition: give up the clutch-plate business for tanks, which was a direct sale under

Backstory: Vermont American

Lee B. Thomas, Sr., who was aware of the growing post-war popularity of power tools and the need for their replacement parts, founded Vermont American initially as American Saw & Tool Co. in 1947. His vision of the first "replacement tool" company began with a single product: a circular saw blade; a single plant: the old American Elevator plant in Louisville, Kentucky; and just one customer: Sears Roebuck & Co. who gave them their first order for 12,000 circular saw blades. With that initial order from Sears, Thomas and his associates originated the manufacturing model for mass-production of the first high-quality, economical circular saw blade, initially using some of the old American Elevator equipment and later using war surplus machines that they adapted for their use. The first shipment of saw blades left Louisville the first week of January 1948, just one month after the order had been received. Vermont American is today the world's largest manufacturer of circular saw blades and power tool accessories.

It is no longer known as Vermont American. A partnership of Robert Bosch and Emerson Electric bought Vermont American in 1989. Bosch later bought out Emerson and combined Vermont American with the Skil Saw operation in Chicago. The combined operation is now known as the Robert Bosch Tool Corporation.

contract to the Army. It's all about planting the seeds of peace. That was my motivation for making such a change.

While I was in charge of Vermont American, I was determined that we would not take war work under contract. If one of our customers wanted to sell to the defense establishment, that was none of our business. We went by this adage, "We know God's will for us, but we don't know God's will for you." We would not use our research and development to create product for the Defense Department. But our distributors could sell products to them if they so chose.

One part of our business was selling industrial tools to distributors, and the bigger part was the do-it-yourself market. But as far as the military contract went, we didn't want to leave the Army high and dry. So I said, "Let's do it right. Give the Army time to find another source. But get rid of it."

My parents disagreed with my position on the military contract, but they never wavered from their support of me. They always said, "Lee, we disagree with you. But we know where you're coming from. We respect you for it, and we'll support you." They knew what kind of experiences I had been through in the war, and knew I had had a strong negative emotional reaction to Hiroshima.

In fact, my dad wrote a beautiful letter on behalf of our son Glenn when he applied for conscientious objector status with his draft board during the war in Vietnam. He and Mother were Episcopalians and strongly supported our Quaker family.

My dad's business partner, Gene Cowley, also disagreed with my decision to get rid of the clutch-plate business. Gene, now deceased, was awarded the Legion of Merit for his design of the pontoon bridge for the Army during World War II. He was a lieutenant colonel in the Army Corps of Engineers and a long-time member of the Army Reserves. But Gene went along with my decision, and he respected me in spite of it – or maybe eventually because of it. Gene was a 100-percent supporter of mine, even though he disagreed with me on some issues. He respected my ability as a manager. Our mutual respect, despite very different views on the morality of the war, existed until the day he passed on.

Meeting Joan, starting a family

At the work camp I met a young woman named Joan Ellwood. She was a student at Swarthmore College, a school founded by the Quakers. She had been working for labor unions for some time and of course I was on the other side: business. But we kept on talking. We talked about a lot of things, including about refusing to pay taxes as a way to protest government spending on the military. But that didn't make much sense. We knew the government would assess a penalty for that. So we determined we would match our income tax payment and give it to charity. It was kind of idealistic for a couple of kids in college.

On a Sunday night, I took her in my arms – the first time I had touched her – kissed her, and asked her to marry me. I had known her for five days. We made a lifetime compact. Later, Joan got her medical degree and served the poor of our city, Louisville, Kentucky, for 21 years. We've been married over 56 years and have had four children – Rees, Glenn, Stephen and Margie. Tragically, Stephen died when he was an infant. Glenn, Margie and Rees all own businesses and they run them ethically. We're very proud of them.

Vietnam protests

In the years to follow I became a pacifist, a position that seemed to threaten the powers-that-be. At Vermont American we employed a man who had once worked for the FBI. He said the agency had two full file drawers on me.

As a Quaker I am against war. So I felt compelled to demonstrate against the Vietnam War.

Quakers have had a tradition of opposing war and are strong pacifists. Although Quakers have no formal creed, there are guiding principles that have helped Quakers bear witness for generations, one of the best known of which is the Peace Testimony. The seminal statement of the Quaker peace witness came from this statement that George Fox wrote in a declaration to Charles II in 1660:

> *We utterly deny all outward wars and strife and fightings with outward weapons, for any end or under any pretence whatsoever. And this is our testimony to the whole world. The spirit of Christ, by which we are guided, is not changeable, so as once to command us from a thing as evil and again to move unto it; and we do certainly know, and so testify to the world, that the spirit of Christ, which leads us into all Truth, will never move us to fight and war against any man with outward weapons, neither for the kingdom of Christ, nor for the kingdoms of this world.*
>
> *At the heart of this Testimony is the conviction that there is something of God in all people. This witnessing to peace can be found in public statements*

and personal reflections, in Quakers' refusal to bear arms in times of civil and international conflict, and in acts of quiet, reconciling diplomacy.

Iraq protests

During the year of anti-war protests on Iraq, 2003, I was standing outside the Catholic Cathedral of the Assumption in Louisville, Kentucky. I was part of a group of war protestors keeping vigil as American and British forces were massing on the border of Iraq poised to invade. I saw a reporter from the local newspaper, *The Courier-Journal,* and I approached him, eager to tell my story.

I told him about how I had seen the devastation at Hiroshima shortly after the atom bomb was dropped there. How war brings only destruction and untold suffering. How we needed to prevent that from happening in Iraq.

"I saw Hiroshima when it was flattened. We don't need to do it again," I told the reporter.

I also organized an anti-war protest at Bellarmine University in Louisville. We gathered on campus, read and prayed. Harsh weather limited the turnout to about 10 of us, but it was a dedicated bunch. The protest was held in the shadow of The Thomas Merton Center on campus. Merton, a Catholic monk, was a man of peace. That's why I am so comfortable working at Bellarmine, where his legacy is preserved for all the world's peacemakers to embrace.

I've spent a lot of time at Bellarmine since I became Executive-in-Residence there in about 1993. In business classes for both undergraduates and graduates, we discuss the ethical dimensions of such topics as takeovers, the conduct of a board of directors, environmental issues, socially responsible investing, and international business.

Backstory: Bellarmine University

Bellarmine University was founded in 1950 as Bellarmine College in Louisville, Kentucky by the Archdiocese of Louisville, following third in a line of diocesan institutions of higher learning founded by this diocese, the oldest in inland America. In 1968, it merged with Louisville's Ursuline College and became an independent university. Today's Bellarmine campus stands on property that was a part of a royal land grant from King George III to James McCorkle for his service in the French and Indian War. When the American Republic was born, Thomas Jefferson, Governor of Virginia, of which Kentucky was then a part, retitled the land.

In 1950, the year of Bellarmine's inception, the new school became one of the first in the Commonwealth of Kentucky open to all races. In 1963, Bellarmine opened the Thomas Merton Studies Center devoted to the works of Thomas Merton, a monk at the Abbey of Gethsemani. Today this internationally significant archive contains over 20,000 pieces in its collection.

I bring up my own experiences and challenge them to think. There is an ecumenical spirit here and I'm happy to be part of it.

Thomas Merton was also extremely ecumenical. He was a personal friend of the Dalai Lama. In fact, he got into trouble with Rome over his willingness to worship with all kinds of people in all kinds of faiths. He lost his life on a trip to worship in the Near East in 1968.

War preparations in 2003 quickened recollections of my own days in the military. Almost 60 years ago, as a combat infantry solider in the Philippines, I discovered that "C" rations are not tasty. When I wasn't on patrol, I cooked the eggs and chickens that I think were stolen from the very people that had suffered from war since the Japanese invasion. We helped to add to the suffering of these people. Desperate women started to appear in and around our encampments. I guess they were so destitute that they were driven to prostitution.

In Iraq today, civilians are suffering huge casualties, just as civilians suffered immensely in the Philippines, Japan and countless other countries embroiled in World War II. When the *Courier-Journal* reporter wrote his story, he identified me as a businessman. I am proud to be an anti-war activist who is also in business. That's a combination you do not often see. I am trying to fulfill my pledge to work for world peace when I left Japan in post-World War II.

Of course, my protests against war were peaceful. My mother's advice comes to mind, "Do not be violent about your nonviolence." War is not the answer. There is no such thing as a just war. That includes the present war in Iraq.

People are frequently trying to get me to accept some kind of "just war theory." I just do not think there is any such thing as a just war.

There is something of God in each of us. If you take another's life, you are destroying something of God. In making the judgment that taking this life is justified, are you not making a judgment that should only be made by God?

When a country embarks on a war that it thinks is justified, it invariably does some horrible things to win that war. In World War II we took an ally, Josef Stalin, who had murdered millions of his own people. We used a weapon to win the war that may at some time in the future destroy the whole planet.

In order to be ready to fight this just war, countries stockpile weapons. They may be hydrogen bombs, biological weapons, or conventional weapons. They all cost money and take away money that might be spent to alleviate suffering.

In my professional life, I have refused to do consulting work for the manufacturers of weapons. The businesses that I have been in do not sell to weapons manufacturers. Some say that I am not patriotic. I think that the highest form of patriotism to your country or to your business is to tell it when you think it is making a mistake. You may say that I am assuming that I know God's will for others. I do not think so. You can buy from our company and resell to whomever you choose. You do not have to work in a company that you find has values that you cannot accept. This is where I stand on the whole issue of the so-called "just war."

Backstory: Just War Theory

Just War Theory concerns the justification—either theoretical or historical—of how and why wars are fought. The theoretical aspect relates to ethically justifying war and forms of warfare. The historical aspect, or the "just war tradition," as old as warfare itself, deals with the historical body of rules or agreements in various wars throughout history (e.g. the Geneva and Hague conventions). Just War Theory offers a series of principles that aim to retain a plausible moral framework for war.

Chapter 3 **Justice**

Open Housing, The Bradens and the KCLU

Carl and Anne Braden were activists promoting open housing in Louisville and it landed them in court. In 1954, they had helped a black family, the Wades, move into an all-white neighborhood in a house on Rone Court (now Clyde Drive). Soon after, a cross was burned in their yard and a bomb was set off at the house, making it uninhabitable and forcing the Wades to move.

Anne Braden was born in 1924 in Louisville but spent her Depression-era childhood in Mississippi and Alabama. After graduating from college in 1945, she became a journalist and returned to Louisville to work for *The Louisville Times*, one of the South's leading liberal newspapers. There she met Carl Braden, a colleague on the paper. Carl, a high-school dropout who had learned his trade on the job, was a radical, the son of an active socialist and railroad worker who had named his son after Karl Marx because he had been "inspired by the Russian Revolution." They married and, through Carl, Anne became involved in a variety of left-wing organizations and causes.

The Bradens are best known for an incident in May, 1954 in which they purchased a ranch-style house in a new, all-white neighborhood of Louisville and, in a pre-arranged transaction meant to protest segregation in housing, resold it to a black family. Neighbors quickly objected to the Bradens' purchase. A month after the new black owners moved in, the house was dynamited.

The following August, the local prosecutor announced his intention to ask a grand jury to investigate the bombing of the house. As a result of their actions, Carl Braden was charged with sedition, since many southern whites interpreted working for racial integration as an outright sign of communist support. He was sentenced to 15 years and served seven months before he was released on the highest bond ever set in Kentucky up to that time. In 1958, the U.S. House Un-American Activities Committee (HUAC) held hearings in Atlanta on "Communist Party propaganda activities in the South" and subpoenaed the Bradens to testify. After Carl refused to answer questions he was convicted of contempt of Congress and sentenced to a year in jail. This time he served the full sentence while Anne campaigned for clemency. In 1967, the Bradens were again charged with sedition for protesting the practice of strip-mining in Pike County, Kentucky. Fortunately, they were able to use this case to test the Kentucky sedition law, which was eventually ruled unconstitutional.

Since her husband's death, Anne has remained active in anti-racist issues. She founded Progress in Education and the Kentucky branch of the Alliance Against Racist and Political Repression to ease the stress of school desegregation in the 1970s, worked on Jesse Jackson's presidential campaign during the 1984 and 1988 elections, and has provided inspiration for many who continue to fight racial injustice.

A grand jury was convened to investigate the incident. This was the McCarthy era – a time when Joe McCarthy and his crowd wrapped themselves up in the American flag while they trampled on individual civil liberties. During this hysterical time, the Bradens were accused of sedition and allegedly involved in a plot to overthrow the government.

I disagreed with the Bradens' politics, but squarely defended their right to legal representation. So when prosecutors went after Carl Braden on a charge of sedition, I put up $500 to help defend him. I saw the effort to prosecute the Bradens as a threat to all liberty-loving people, including Quakers.

Remember what the Rev. Martin Niemoeller said of his experiences in Hitler's Germany:

> *First they came for the Communists, but I was not a Communist so I did not speak out. Then they came for the Socialists and the Trade Unionists, but I was neither, so I did not speak out. Then they came for the Jews, but I was not a Jew so I did not speak out. And when they came for me, there was no one left to speak out for me.*

But unfortunately, the prosecution prevailed and Carl Braden went to prison for seven months. The conviction was later overturned. In fact, his prosecutors were my brother-in-law at the time, Scott Hamilton, and his father. (Later when I was embroiled in the Vermont American trial, Scott got up and told the judge, "I've disagreed with Lee on a lot of things, but if Lee tells you something, you can take it to the bank.")

I was the first person to provide financial backing to form the Kentucky Civil Liberties Union. But I ended up resigning from the board due to my differences with Anne Braden. I wanted to support the civil liberties of all people

– the extreme right, the extreme left, and those in the middle – and I was afraid their support of civil liberties would be politically motivated.

Flashback: Focus on the family

"One reason I went to work at Vermont American was the value that the company placed on your time. There was more to life than work. Family was valued and honored. If there was any way you could get home to dinner, you were supposed to do that. If there was any way you were able to travel only three days a week instead of four so you could be with your family, that was an expectation. You were to try to maximize your focus on productivity so you did not neglect other things. The allocation of your time was where you honored all the commitments in your life – family, community, church, parents, etc."

— *Olivia Kirtley*
Vice President of Finance
Vermont American

Chapter 4 **Ethics**

Ethical concerns as a CPA

After earning an industrial engineering degree from Yale, I went to work for Touche Ross Bailey Smart CPAs (now Deloitte & Touche) in Chicago. As a consultant and a Quaker, I asked not to be assigned to work with companies that were involved in the military industrial complex. Jackson Smart, my boss at the firm and my mentor, backed me up 100 percent. He said, "I disagree with you, but we'll accommodate you because we need people of principle around here."

I was managing audits for the accounting firm. I was also doing consulting work in the summer, and going to night school at Northwestern University to get my CPA.

We're reading about that today in the Arthur Andersen case. The fact is, Mr. Smart would never let anybody who had ever done any consulting work get close to a company doing the audit. They were absolutely separate; there was a wall in between. Mr. Smart had ethics.

I was the manager on an appliance manufacturer audit toward the end of my career there. It was after the Korean War and steel was on allocation by the government. Legally you could buy more than your allocation, but you paid a huge premium for it. According to the rules of accountancy, you have to write that off, meaning cancel it from the account as a loss. You don't keep that on your books because

41

it's the lower of cost of market and if you wanted to sell that steel after the war, obviously you couldn't get that premium for it. So I discovered the premium still on the books.

I called the partner in Detroit and he said, "We can't write it off because the client is very adamant about it and we don't want to lose the customer." I went to Mr. Smart and briefed him on the situation. He said, "Lee, you're exactly right. You get out of the middle of this one. I'll handle it." We didn't lose the customer; we lost the partner. He went on to head up a major American corporation, which ended up nearly going bankrupt.

So how does my story relate to the Enron era? When you're an auditor, the public is looking to you to give an honest evaluation of what this company can do. You're not supposed to be thinking about how you can keep the customer. Talk about sin run wild. That's just awful, and of course it's what Arthur Andersen was doing.

Too many of these so-called "Chinese walls" – supposedly between auditing and management consulting – are made of Swiss cheese.

A "Chinese wall" is an ethical barrier or zone of non-communication between different divisions of a business to prevent conflict of interest." The term was coined following the stock market crash of 1929 when the U.S. government sought to provide a barrier between investment bankers and brokerage firms as effective as the 1,500 miles-long Great Wall of China. Despite Chinese walls, many circumstances of conflict of interest occurred during the recent "dot com" days during which research analysts marketed companies in which they, or related parties, owned shares. By circulating positive research advice, or even simply by choosing to talk about their client among the thousands of possible companies they might have discussed, the share price of these companies was elevated without regard for actual financial worthiness. This was one of the factors contributing to the dot com "bubble" which eventually burst around the first half of 2000. The U.S. government has since passed laws such as the Sarbanes-Oxley Act (officially titled the Public Company Accounting Reform and Investor Protection Act of 2002 and commonly called SOX and Sarbox) to improve the Chinese wall concept.

Today, I think it's easier to stand tall. The facts speak for themselves: Enron is gone. Arthur Andersen is no more. The other CPA firms have got to learn something from this. I believe that if you come off an audit and there's something you don't like and you stand tall, you're going to be respected today. My experience with the washing machine audit taught me a whole lot about ethics, about being strong and standing up for my principles.

Vermont American

I was already manager of the accounting firm and was headed for a partnership, but I was traveling so much that it was interfering with my family life. And Dad was after me to come into the business in Louisville. He made a deal with me. He said, "Lee, I will always be candid with you. I'll always tell you what I think. But if you take bad advice from me, then you're the damned fool and I will stick to it." And with that, I came to Louisville to work with Vermont American.

Dad had been president of Ekco Products of Chicago (now a division of World Kitchens, Inc.). He came to Louisville in the mid-1940s to manage a small company,

American Elevator and Machine Co. That company was in deep financial trouble and was facing bankruptcy. Dad restructured the company and proceeded to straighten it out. The owners saw the shrinking company and made a deal with Dad.

Dad took the little circular saw company that they had started in a corner of the plant. It was subject to a preferred stock interest and a lease. The old owners, the Phillips family, took the elevator repair business that was all that was left of the American Elevator and Machine Co., and the building. It was all done amicably, and the Thomases and Phillipses remained friends throughout their lives.

Dad's little company was American Saw and Tool, the original entity that would become Vermont American Corp. The Sears, Roebuck & Company was having trouble getting circular saws. Vermont American traced its roots to 1947 or 1948 when my dad received the first order for 12,000 circular saw blades from Sears. Sears' source for the saw blades had been meeting with competitors and fixing prices, and Sears could not get a discount even though Sears was their biggest purchaser at that time. Then the source built a fancy office building and gave big perks to management. The employees got mad and went on strike.

That's when Sears came to Dad and asked if he could manufacture circular saws. Dad asked Gene Cowley about it. Gene was the chief engineer for American Elevator and Machine Co. and left there to join Dad to start American Saw and Tool. He replied, "Sure!" and went to work inventing the first automated saw manufacturing plant in the world. This was amazing in that he had never even seen a circular saw made.

The smartest decision we ever made at Vermont American was to pay Gene Cowley a tad bit more than the board was paying me even though I was the CEO. I even made sure that he reported directly to the Board of Directors just like I did instead of reporting to me. He was making the biggest contribution to the business and he was worth more than I was. Dad had inherited a genius.

In fact, Gene and his colleague Mac McCord invented virtually everything new that came along in the power-tool business. We were the first company to make a carbide-tip saw for the consumer. It was common for industrial use, but it took creativity to get it down to sell under $10 for household use. We were also the first people to use titanium nitrate coating. There they had considerable help from our son Glenn, who had written his thesis on surface chemistry and had research experience with high-vacuum equipment. These and other innovations made the company grow rapidly, and succeed.

Gene Cowley was an icon in the history of the tool industry. In an article written by Bill Brockway, with Rick Schwolsky and Mark Clement for their *Tools of the Trade* magazine, January/February 2002, they described one of the ways Gene's inventive approach changed the way we now work with tools:

> *Carbide was invented in Germany in the 1920s. Easily machined, super hard, and able to hold an edge, its potential was quickly apparent. It was introduced at an industrial fair in 1927 and bore the trade name "Widia," meaning "like diamonds."*
>
> *Until the late 1940s, carbide-tipped circular saw*

blades were used almost exclusively for cutting metal. The carbide tips were brazed onto the teeth by hand and the saw plates were also flattened or tuned by hand. An eight-tooth blade cost $60 or more at that time.

In 1950, Gene Cowley examined a German-made, eight-tooth, carbide-tipped saw blade that retailed for $41. He set himself a nearly impossible task — produce a blade of equal or better quality for one quarter of the price. Knowing he'd need some help, Cowley hired engineer Mac McCord. Under Cowley's leadership, they designed machines to cut and flatten blade blanks, braze carbide tips onto the blade teeth, and grind the tips to uniform width and razor sharpness. The automation increased production speed and lowered costs. In late 1951, Vermont American shipped the first carbide-tipped blades to market. The eight-tooth blades retailed for $9.99.

After a couple of years as Sears' source, Gene and Dad went to them and acknowledged they were making too much money on the circular saws. They wanted to cut the price before somebody else forced them to do so, thereby creating a barrier to entry into the market by our competitors. Bob Dyer of Sears said Sears was aware of it, and said a price change would be made in a year. Dyer told them to make improvements to the company operation with the extra money in the meantime in order to be able to handle the increased order volume. This was my first introduction to partnerships! The system does work to everyone's advantage when there is competition.

Barriers to Entry

Barriers to entry are obstacles placed in the path of a firm that wants to enter a given market. The economist Joseph Stigler defined an entry barrier as a cost of producing (at some or every rate of output) which must be borne by a firm that seeks to enter an industry but is not borne by firms already in the industry.

Some examples of barriers to entry are:

• Legal protection through patents to produce a product for a number of years;

• Pricing policies that lower prices to a level that would force any new entrants to operate at a loss;

• Lower costs, perhaps through experience of being in the market for some time, allowing the existing product's producer to cut prices and win price wars;

• Consumer loyalty of the existing product that makes successful entry into the market by new firms much more expensive;

• Trade restrictions such as tariffs and quotas.

Vermont American was a powerhouse of innovation in steel and circular saw blades and router bits. Those were the things that made the company the largest power tool accessory manufacturer in the world. We made Sears' Craftsman brand, the Master Mechanic brand, our own brand. We didn't care what label we put on it. We were serving a need for the consumer, and how we satisfied that need was the important thing.

In 1961, we bought Vermont Tap and Die Co. of Lyndonville, Vt., and renamed the company Vermont American Corp.

I joined Vermont American in 1954 when I was 28 years old. I was underemployed for a while. Then gradually, I started getting extra responsibilities, including purchasing and labor relations. In 1962, at the age of 36-years-old, I was named Chief Executive Officer of Vermont American. The company then had $9 million in annual sales. By the time we sold out in 1989, the company had $450 million in sales and was in the ranks of the Fortune 1000.

We were in a high-growth industry. As its dominant player, we regularly communicated with stock analysts who monitored us and tried to develop a good relationship with them. Illustrating the fact that we were rapidly growing, I told this joke to a group of these analysts in the 1960s:

> A doctor hired a plumber to fix a backup. It took the plumber only 30 seconds with the plunger to fix the problem. When the doctor got a bill for $56, he was irate, and called the plumber to complain. The plumber explained the bill was so high because it was a Sunday house call. The doctor said, "I don't get that kind of money for a house call," to which the plumber replied, "I didn't either when I was a doctor."

The entrepreneurial spirit is created when people are forced to take action themselves. Vermont American's talented, ethical managers were responsible for our phenomenal growth. They, not I, are the true entrepreneurs.

Chapter 5 **Honesty**

Firing the consultants

I got lucky. The first time I challenged management at American Saw & Tool, Co., I was right. At the time I was the purchasing agent and had just received responsibility for labor relations. We had had a strike at the old American Saw and Tool Co. plant in Louisville and somehow or another the way it was settled didn't pass the smell test. All of a sudden the strike was over. Something was wrong. So I did an investigation on the consulting firm that was working with us.

The firm was Nathan Shefferman's organization, Labor Relations Associates of Chicago. Our biggest customer, Sears, had recommended them to us. I started digging. I wrote a letter to the clerk of the 57th Street Friends Meeting (Quakers) in Chicago, Garfield Cox. Garfield was also dean of the School of Business at the University of Chicago. Joan and I had been members of the 57th Street Meeting when we lived in that city. I asked Garfield to evaluate Labor Relations Associates.

Garfield wrote back a letter in classic Quaker terminology. He said, "Lee, I think over a period of time a conscientious management would find the association a difficult one." On his word alone as my trusted mentor, I fired Labor Relations Associates. I went in and told my dad and the president of the company, John Beam, what I had done. Dad had told me if I made a decision, he'd stand by me. And he was good to his word.

A word about Nathan W. Shefferman

Nathan W. Shefferman (1887 – 1968) pioneered the modern anti-union consulting industry. His first job was with the American Institute of Phrenology, where he presumably learned to associate personalities and mental abilities with the shapes and sizes of subjects' heads. After World War II, American management began to hire individuals like Shefferman who claimed backgrounds in industrial psychology, management, and labor law, as their new anti-union weapons.

Labor Relations Associates of Chicago, Inc., formed under the auspices of Sears, Roebuck and Company and led by Shefferman, became the leading anti-labor consulting firm paid by their employers to help them defeat unionization movements. Shefferman used both legal and illegal tactics to fight union organizing drives. In the late 1950s, Congressional scrutiny of Shefferman's activities and his close relationship with Teamsters Union president Dave Beck (to whom Shefferman had made illegal payments to head off Teamster organizing) led to the passage of the Labor Management Reporting and Disclosure Act (the Landrum-Griffin Act). The new law required management to report agreements with labor relations consultants and required unions to "open their books."

But when I took that action, you never heard silence so thick. You could cut it with a knife. "What the hell do you know about labor relations?" Dad and John asked. I answered that I had taken one course on labor relations in college, which gave me just about enough knowledge to be dangerous.

I called upon my friend Wight Bakke from Yale for help with our labor relations. Wight knew every labor leader in this country. He'd helped set up the school for industrial relations in Egypt, in Norway and Delhi, India. The guy knew more about labor relations than anyone else in the world, and I called him and told him my problem. He said, "Oh, sure, I'll take you on." I went to Yale to see him.

Eighteen months after I fired Nathan Shefferman, the Senate Rackets Committee exposed them, and Dave Beck, the president of the Teamsters Union, went to jail. Labor Relations Associates was working both sides of the street. So I got the opportunity to wear the white hat.

Unfortunately there were a lot of companies in Louisville that didn't have the opportunity to wear the white hat. They were Shefferman's clients, too, and fell victim to the consultant's dishonest dealings. But they were not as lucky as we were. After that I could make mistakes and get away with them. Doing the right thing: that was what it was all about.

In business as in life, honesty should be our guiding force. If you are honest, you don't have to second-guess your actions. You don't have to look over your shoulder. Honest, straightforward dealings. That's been a hallmark in the life of our businesses – Vermont American and Universal Woods.

Flashback: Paying the penalty
"One time around Christmas time Lee went on

vacation and somebody put on his desk some personal tax filing that was required. But he didn't get back until after the deadline. It would never have occurred to him to backdate that form to avoid paying the penalty. His philosophy was, that's less money I have to give to charity because my net is less. The penalty was substantial, but he paid it.

"Lesson: You don't evaluate what's right to do by how much it will cost. I think Lee did that in all areas of business. For so many people, the first filter is, 'How much is it going to cost in either time or money or reputation?' Lee would forgive you many times over if you could do things better in time or money, but there wasn't much forgiveness if people didn't do what was right."

— *Olivia Kirtley*
Vice President of Finance
Vermont American

Tell the truth always

When you do business with a nogoodnik, you end up paying for it. That was the harsh lesson learned when I bought Universal Woods in 1990. I signed a five-year contract with the former CEO to continue to serve as president of the company. He had invented the manufacturing process that we used, and had strong personal relationships with customers and suppliers. We needed him to keep things operating.

But the Universal Corporation didn't reveal that he had a serious health problem. He was a heavy smoker and was running out of lung capacity. His doctor refused to do

Backstory: Universal Woods

Universal Woods in Louisville, Kentucky is a leader in coating and sublimation technologies, the process by which an image printed on paper is transferred to another surface (or substrate.) Historically, sublimation has been used for t-shirts, tiles and metal plaques. With more than 35 years in the finishing industry, Universal Woods has pioneered a 15-step process that allows the transferred image to become part of the substrate, not just sit on top of it, creating a longer lasting and more durable product. Purchased by Lee Thomas in 1990 and run by Paul Neumann, Universal Woods is a business that has put the Quaker values of its executives into action through their integrity in dealing with customers, suppliers, and employees, support of diversity in their work force, paying wages and providing healthcare benefits that allow their employees and families to have a reasonable standard of living, and employing environmentally friendly manufacturing and coating technologies.

surgery. This man's days were numbered. So after only two years he was forced by poor health to take early retirement, and passed away soon afterward.

I was stuck. It left me in a terrible dilemma.

That experience reminds me of reading about the three standards of truth:

1.   Legal truth: If it isn't perjury, it's true.

2.   Conveying the truth. President Clinton didn't pass that test when he was talking about Monica Lewinsky – and look where it got him!

3.   But the Rabbi Gaon, writing in the sixth century, addressed "Truth in Silence," the standard we follow. He said that you are obliged to disclose information that the person across the table from you needs to make a good decision, even if it's not in your best financial interest. (She'Elot of Rav Ahai Gaon Parashat Vayechi #36)

The law is very clear that if you have a basement that leaks and you have a home for sale, you've got to tell prospective buyers about that. The law is very clear that if you have an automobile and it's been in a wreck and you go to trade it in, you've got to tell them. That's the law.

But there wasn't any law that said somebody had to disclose their health condition – even if that could have had a negative impact on the other party. That's where ethics come in. An ethical person would not think twice about owning up to the truth, even if it hurts him or her in their business dealings.

Hiring ethical, independently minded employees

Nowhere in business is it more important to promote

honesty than among your employees. A CEO needs men and women of high ethical standards who will tell the truth always.

One such ethical man is Paul Neumann who runs Universal Woods. (Read more about Paul in Chapter 11: Partnerships.) Another of these impeccably honest men was George Chapman who served as vice president of manufacturing at American Saw & Tool and then Vermont American. If there ever was a guy who would tell me I was crazy when I needed to hear that, it was George. If you surround yourself with people who tell you how great you are, you can't do a good job of managing. A person who keeps telling you how great you are is either stupid or fixing to skin you! My job was not to develop a culture of "yes" people. You don't reach consensus when everybody says the same thing, but by listening to what everybody's got to say. Profits, stocks and price earnings weren't the driving force 100 percent of the time. They take care of themselves when you take care of your people and all of the stakeholders.

George was from Great Britain. He got his MBA and started working for one of our Vermont American plants. When somebody wasn't getting the job done, they reported to George for awhile, and he would help them get back on track. George was a hands-on manager.

One day he quit and bought a circular saw company from the Triangle Corp., in Shelbyville, Kentucky. Overnight he became a competitor. But when he left, he didn't take anything with him – except the knowledge in his head. He left under totally honorable conditions, and was an honest competitor.

After a year or two, George and a business partner had

a falling-out, and he was back looking for work. He wrote me asking if he could use my name as a reference. I didn't answer his letter. Instead, I was in his driveway waiting for him to come home that night – and I hired him right back. Why? Because a guy who tells you you're going to make a mistake is the most valuable person you can have .

Firing unethical employees

The flip side of hiring honest, straight-talking employees is firing employees who are unethical and dishonest, if not engaged in unlawful acts.

A CEO's moral, ethical and legal obligation is to provide employees with a harassment-free work place. Our auditors had heard there was a problem with sexual harassment within our company. They put a questionnaire on employees' desks that asked, "Should we spend any time looking for sexual harassment?" It directed employees to check yes or no, and return the questionnaires. They didn't have to sign them.

The auditors got some "yes" responses. They determined who the culprit was and found his desk full of dirty pictures. He was harassing the women in the place. They had him dead-to-rights. This was a fellow who had sold us his business and we had kept him on to run it. He was active politically. We fired him. Then we made sure the company knew about the unacceptable behavior. The employee in question had damaged not only himself, but also the company and all his co-workers. We had to let everyone know we wouldn't stand for it; we wouldn't allow it and didn't want to be associated with this kind of behavior.

In another case, we had a competent executive who was a division president. He had had an affair with his secretary. Ordinarily, what a person does on his own time is his own business. In this case, however, he had power over his secretary and that made it wrong. She'd already quit her job and their relationship was apparently consensual, but that made no difference. He had to go. He had to find another job.

We didn't fire him outright. We told him, "You've done a good job. We like you. But there's a problem. You're going to have to find another job. Take your time. You're still working here. If you need to take time off for an interview, go ahead. Help us to train your replacement." He found another job – as a purchasing agent for one of our customers. We hadn't made an enemy. He continued to buy our merchandise. It was the humane approach to firing somebody and it turned out to be a good business decision.

Sexual Harassment

The U.S. Supreme Court recognized sexual harassment as a practice of sex discrimination in 1986. It is illegal because it violates Title VII of the Civil Rights Act of 1964. Unwelcome sexual advances, requests for sexual favors, and other verbal or physical conduct of a sexual nature constitutes sexual harassment when submission to or rejection of this conduct explicitly or implicitly affects an individual's employment, unreasonably interferes with an individual's work performance or creates an intimidating, hostile or offensive work environment.

Sexual harassment can occur in a variety of circumstances, including but not limited to the following:

• The victim as well as the harasser may be a woman or a man. The victim does not have to be of the opposite sex;

• The harasser can be the victim's supervisor, an agent of the employer, a supervisor in another area, a co-worker, or a non-employee;

• The victim does not have to be the person harassed but could be anyone affected by the offensive conduct;

• Unlawful sexual harassment may occur without economic injury to or discharge of the victim.

• Sexual harassment is illegal at work and school because that is where sex equality is legally guaranteed, not because there is no sexual harassment in other places in society.

Another time, we caught an employee stealing from our credit union. We fired him right away, but declined to press charges after his father made restitution. Then we heard that one of our suppliers needed a warehouse worker. We told the supplier the whole story. They said the job did not involve handling money, and didn't mind giving this man a second chance.

There are different ways to fire unethical employees. Our goal is not to make an enemy or destroy a person's life. We try to help them get back on their feet when possible. It's the right thing to do.

Honesty lays the groundwork for partnerships and mutual respect. That especially holds true in labor relations. In more than 50 years at two companies, Vermont American and Universal Woods, we have had extraordinary relations with our employees.

That was no accident.

Flashback: Dishonesty kills a deal

"We were looking to buy a toolbox company in Phoenix. As part of the audit we did our due diligence and walked around the building. They were pouring paint residue into the sand in the back of the building and it was going directly into the water system. We were real close to buying the place, but Lee was adamant. He said, 'Just pack up and come home. We're not buying it.'"

— Shane Jones
Internal Audit Director and
Distribution Center Manager
Vermont American

Chapter 6 **Consensus**

Developing good labor relations

You will find mentors in your life if you are open to receive them. And sometimes they appear in the most unlikely places.

In the late 1950s, I hired Bob Sutherland to handle labor relations at American Saw & Tool, our dominant plant at the time. Bob had gone to the Southern Baptist Theological Seminary, but he became disenchanted and left. He was told that his questioning of dogma was heretical. Before he joined us, he went to work in a factory and became chief steward for the union, leading them through a strike. He did a great job, helping to improve morale at Vermont American. At the same time, we made improvements, going from individual piece rate to group incentives.

Bob had relevant experience, albeit on the other side of the management-labor divide from me. He was thoroughly ethical. He made the people in the factory his flock. He wanted to be a minister and, by golly, he was one. He was also a mentor, even though he reported to me. The key question is what kind of relationship do you have with your people? Bob knew how to do it. You've got to have a relationship with your people that's loving. Otherwise nothing goes.

Unions mostly live by being contentious, so I have no problem at all trying to manage the business so that the employees don't want a union, or they don't need a union. But you're not always going to accomplish that, particularly in a decentralized business. Your objective as a manager dealing with a union is to develop a non-contentious relationship as best you can. Honesty is the key thing.

In 1961, Vermont Tap & Die Co. was for sale. The owner was an 80-year-old despot who wasn't equipped to deal with a union, but that's the direction the workers were heading – whether the owner liked it or not. These circumstances presented our company with an opportunity to buy Vermont Tap & Die.

We all recognized that there was no way we were going to keep the union out. The workers had a choice between the communist-dominated United Electrical Workers of America, and the steelworkers union, United Steelworkers of America. I suggested that we try to get the steelworkers to win that election.

That's what we did and Wight Bakke helped us. We talked them up, saying we could do business with Tom Breslin, the steelworkers' international representative. Tom had never seen anything like this in all of his life. As a union man, he was expecting a contentious situation, but he didn't get it. The steelworkers easily won the election and then we sat down to talk. Wight was at the head of the table and served as "clerk," a Quaker term that refers to the facilitator of meeting for business.

Tom had worked with some Quakers at the Civil Liberties Union and had learned a little something about consensus building. The president of the local union was a lay Methodist minister and he knew all about consensus.

Backstory: Clerk of a Quaker Meeting

In traditional Quaker worship, there are no pastors, rituals, or programmed activities such as readings or music. Worship is held "on the basis of silence," so that all worshipers may, in unity with all those assembled, open their minds and hearts to the leading of the divine Spirit.

The Meeting is served by a Presiding Clerk, and often also by a Recording Clerk. Friends are appointed for a limited time, and these roles are shared among the membership of the Meeting. The Clerks have no formal authority. Their task is to focus and enable the discernment of the Meeting by laying business before it in an orderly way, managing the pace and discipline of discussions, listening for the sense of the Meeting to emerge, restating that sense in clear language and asking for approval, and recording the business in written minutes.

When things started to get heated, we actually sat in silence in our labor negotiations much like Quakers sit in silence during our Meetings for Business. In this way we tried to achieve consensus instead of yelling and screaming at each other.

It was far different than any labor relations that Tom or I had seen. The strong cooperative relationship between labor and management lasted for 30-odd years.

Flashback: Silence guides decision-making

"We had a general manager who was terrible to everyone. He played employees off of each other and treated everyone badly. Lee said this guy was just in the wrong position and he would try moving him around. Lee came to our plant. He used a Quaker format to reconcile the situation. Everyone sat around silently for a long time. There was no finger pointing. By the end of the day they decided this manager had other strong points and honestly wanted the business to thrive. The man ended up admitting he was in the wrong position, so Lee put him elsewhere. Lee was a facilitator for change. I learned from this experience that many business decisions don't have to be made on the spot. It's not a sign of weakness to delay a decision."

— Nat Campbell III
Boone Plant Manager and
European Sales and
Marketing Director
Vermont American

Backstory: Quakers and Consensus

Consensus is a way to make decisions without voting. A belief in common humanity and the ability to decide together are key components of Quaker-based consensus, the goal being unity, not unanimity. The group works together to agree on the best decision that everyone can support. The Quaker model works well when employed in secular settings because it gives everyone a chance to speak while limiting potential disruptors.

The following characteristics of the Quaker model are often effectively applied in non-Quaker consensus decision-making processes:

Multiple concerns and information are shared until the sense of the group is clear;

Discussion involves active listening and sharing of information;

Norms limit number of times one asks to speak to ensure that each speaker is fully heard;

Ideas and solutions belong to the group; no names are recorded;

Differences are resolved by discussion. The facilitator identifies areas of agreement and names disagreements to push discussion deeper;

The group as a whole is responsible for the decision, and the decision belongs to the group;

Dissenters' perspectives are embraced.

Around the late 1970s, the economy was weak and competition got tougher for Vermont Tap & Die, a plant that made industrial cutting tools. Many factories were moving south, but we didn't follow suit. We had to do something, so I went to the union at the plant and told them that we needed a 12 percent giveback. We were being forced to cut wages and benefits by 12 percent. This was a big concession on their part, but out of a couple hundred union workers, there were only two negative votes.

We could only accomplish that because we had excellent communications between labor and management. The relationship was remarkable – and rare in the world of business.

In about 1981, business was not good and we had to make some adjustments at our Multi-Metals plant. Rather than lay off salaried employees, we reduced salaries by 10 percent on the plant level for three months. At the end of four months, business had recovered and we went on as usual.

We had to do some things to control our costs. In business you have choices about what you do. What may inform your choices is a concern for people. The payback for the company is their continuing dedication to the company.

Today, as the economy is getting more competitive and business is becoming more global, it's more and more important for astute management to ensure that they are communicating with employees.

Keeping plants small and caring for employees

At Vermont American we purposely kept our plants small, usually less than 300 people. We'd simply open a new plant making the same product if a plant had more employees than 300. We wanted to build personal relationships with our employees.

Some companies argue that with a larger plant, they can spread your overhead over a lot more people and volume, thus reducing costs. But I believe larger plants might hinder customer service. Larger plants mean less oversight over the quality, production and process that benefit your customer. Also, you may have a greater degree of turnover, and that's costly.

Handling layoffs at the company

I have a big problem with a CEO who downsizes his company while raking in big bonuses. That's just invidious. The first thing a CEO should do before scaling down an operation is to take a salary cut and require that management do the same. But I'm getting ahead of my story.

In the late 1970s, Vermont American had to close a couple of plants. This was a terrible time for everybody. One of the plants was the company's original American Saw & Tool plant on Main Street in Louisville.

Here's how we handled it: I took a 10 percent cut and took no bonus that year. Everyone making over $35,000 a year took a five percent cut. Then we closed three plants. We kept the personnel department here in Louisville. Its sole responsibility was to find people jobs. We let people transfer within the company where possible. I went through and talked to every single employee. We got jobs for all but five of them, and those five had substance abuse problems. There were 140 employees affected in that plant alone. Unfortunately, most employees got jobs paying less than what they were making with us.

Three years later, American Saw & Tool employees had a reunion, and they invited me to attend. I had failed them and I cried. I wasn't able to figure out a way to keep the plant open and those people employed. But they forgave me. They knew we had no other choice but to close that plant. That taught me a powerful lesson: treat people with dignity and respect in good times and bad. If they believe you did everything you could for them, they will still hold you in high regard.

Layoffs: Bad for business

In the more than a dozen years since I acquired Universal Woods, we haven't had a single layoff. Even during down times, we give our employees – and we're all employees, including me – the choice between taking a vacation day or keeping busy around the shop. The cost of a layoff is huge. You lose your better people. When you recall the furloughed work force, the better people have already found jobs elsewhere. You get back the people you'd just as soon not get back.

And from a business standpoint, layoffs are very expensive. Layoffs are sometimes necessary, as our experience at Vermont American bears out. But at Universal Woods, we have an egalitarian philosophy: we're in this mess together.

We had a significant slowdown after 9-11. We had about three weeks of work to do in a four-week month. We could have done the classic thing – work three weeks and lay people off for a week. Essentially the employees bear the costs and we reduce our costs. Then you hope they return to work after the short layoff.

But the upshot of that would have been that the

employees could not claim unemployment and that would have been unfair to them. Instead, we reached this deal: we worked a four-day week. Then they could take the fifth day off without pay or we would pay a half-day if they would use a half-day of vacation time. This helped us through a four-month stretch of business. When the business bounced back, we had been able to handle the problem without a significant disruption in our work force or undue hardship on our employees.

Drawing no distinctions

In what ways are we egalitarian? Most in the factory are guaranteed a 40-hour week— highly unusual in a manufacturing setting.

Ordinarily, when a factory employee is off sick, he or she is not paid. If somebody is off for whatever reason at Universal Woods, they're paid. One man who had prostate cancer surgery was off five weeks – and he got paid his full salary. People in the office are paid a salary, so why should it be any different for people on the factory floor?

We have no union at Universal Woods and we hope our employees don't want one. They'd have to do away with the salary program and they're content with it. We also have one 401(k) retirement plan and the same health insurance for everyone. In the business world, it's more typical to establish one health plan for management and another for the workers. Our turnover is small. As far as absenteeism, our daily average is two percent, much lower than for many other manufacturing firms.

Ethics is good business. That's the beauty of it. People want to work with you when they're respected and taken care of.

Flashback: Caring for employees

"I remember the first time we co-paid on medical. We had discussions about it for probably at least three months. We went round and round discussing whether the people could afford it. But medical costs rose something like 400 percent at the time. The company paid all medical premiums at first, and then we went to $10 co-pays. This type of thing really concerned Vermont American. We always explained everything to the workers and didn't just push things on them."

— Tim Shea
Vice President of Finance and
later President
Vermont American

Abortion coverage for employees

We've always tried to run our business by staying in close touch with employees. Some call it management by walking around. I like to call it management by listening to other people.

In the late 1970s, after the Roe v. Wade ruling, I had reservations whether our group health-care plan ought to be paying for abortion. We were self-insured and it was entirely our option. I felt abortion was a personal choice and I wasn't sure everybody else should be paying for it. I was talking about modifying the plan. I had visits from many employees who contended I was trying to impose my values on other people. They were very much opposed to my position. They convinced me to retain this health-care coverage, even though I was unhappy about it.

I don't like abortion. But I don't propose to know God's will for other people, and that was the point they were making, and they were right. They convinced me.

Flashback: Staying in touch with the workers

"Lee wanted to build a team of people to make decisions themselves, who have compassion for people who work for them. He spread the philosophy that we listen to everybody from the floor sweeper on up and that we treat them with dignity. When Lee would visit a plant, he wouldn't stop in the office first, he would visit the factory for two or three hours, first talking to the machine operators then go to the office. The managers were supposed to spend at least three hours a day on the factory floor. Once or twice a month managers came in during the second or third shift to stay in touch with the employees. Top management had genuine concern for all levels of employees. Two-way communication was not only encouraged, it was required."

— George Chapman
General Manager and
Vice President of Manufacturing
American Saw & Tool

Chapter 7 **Diversity**

Promoting differences: The right thing to do

I don't like the limelight. My faith teaches me to live a plain and simple life. So I've felt uncomfortable when the compliments start to fly and the congratulations are laid on thick and heavy.

A notable exception came in 2004 when my wife Joan and I were jointly awarded the Arthur M. Walters Champion of Diversity Award from the Louisville Urban League. Joan and I have supported this organization for more than 50 years. Many times in my business career, the Urban League referred capable African-Americans to us for employment.

When we got the award, I asked two people to stand up and be recognized: Alonzo Crumes and Carroll Price. These two men, both African-Americans, were sales managers for Vermont American in the early 1970s. They were the first people of color to have that responsibility in this part of the country, and they were successful at it. If they had not been as successful, the company would not have been as successful. During my remarks upon accepting this award I said, "If these two guys hadn't sold the hell out of Vermont American merchandise, Joan would be here by herself tonight!" You're only as good as the people around you.

I am a radical on diversity. When I was Vermont

Backstory: The Arthur M. Walters Champion of Diversity Award

The Arthur M. Walters Champion of Diversity Award of the Louisville Urban League recognizes outstanding achievement by an individual, business or organization in the promotion of diversity within the Louisville community. The nominees for this award are examined for the extent to which they:

• Make an effort to cultivate relationships with people of different racial, ethnic, religious, gender, cultural and socio-economic groups;

• Examine their own corporate philosophies and initiatives or individual attitudes and behaviors to become more aligned with principles of diversity and inclusion;

• Initiate corrective action to eliminate discriminatory policies and or practices;

• Take a positive stand for equality and empowerment of the disadvantaged within our community;

• Publicly display visual evidence of support for efforts to encourage inclusion, eliminate discrimination/prejudice and/or promote diversity;

• Support an agency, fund, or program that actively works toward the empowerment of disadvantaged groups within our community;

• Actively promote diversity and inclusion within political arenas;

• Seek to learn about the importance of diversity and inclusion;

• Demonstrate a commitment to supporting minority-owned businesses;

• Teach educational programs that promote inclusion and appreciation of diversity;

• Set positive examples toward promoting diversity by both actions and words on a daily consistent basis.

American CEO, I marched with Martin Luther King, Jr. In fact, I kept his picture hanging in my company office (right alongside Gandhi's). This was the 1960s and it turned a few heads! I will not tolerate anything less than a proactive approach to diversity. This includes all kinds of diversity – political, racial, gender, nationality, sexual orientation, etc.

In 1966, I integrated an all-black group, the American Bridge Association, at a national bridge tournament in Louisville. There were 1,500 players from all over the hemisphere. Fourteen hundred and ninety nine of them were black, and there was me. They could not play in the exclusively white American Contract Bridge League, but they welcomed me, a white man, into their league. I got acquainted with educated, cultured African-Americans from all across this country. I had broken the color barrier in a game. But a decade earlier Vermont American integrated the work force at a time when it was not all that common.

Business goals and personal values should not be mutually exclusive. As a Quaker, I believe there is that of God in everyone. That has helped to drive my views on diversity – especially when it came to the hiring of women and African-Americans at a time that many if not most businesses weren't really giving them much of a chance to come into the mainstream.

In the 1950s at Vermont American all the material handlers were African-American. There were no blacks in production or managerial positions. Our plant superintendent brought in his neighbor, a white man, to fill a vacant position as a material handler. The African-American on the union committee said we couldn't hire a white man for a black man's job without being able to hire a black man for a white man's job. That opened up the channels of communication on the issue. Without waiting on its leadership to take action, the union committee held a meeting at the union hall. Afterward they announced: "OK, let's integrate the place."

Chinese philosopher Lao-Tsu, speaking about 600 B.C., said, "To lead the people, walk behind them." The best work is done when people can say, "We did it ourselves."

Later, I wanted to place blacks in managerial jobs. But not everybody in the company saw things the way I did. Some objections arose from the union and the white-dominated management, but they were spotty and restricted to very few. Most people simply lacked the courage to make such a change.

One executive approached me and objected to integrating management ranks. "I just cannot live with this," this executive said. I responded, "Well, Bill, we're going to miss you. I hate to see you leave." He ended up staying on.

Earlier I mentioned Alonzo Crumes. (Gene Cowley was a big supporter of Alonzo's and, in fact, a champion of our racial diversity program at Vermont American.) Alonzo handled sales in Kentucky, Southern Indiana and Southern Ohio. Soon after we hired him, we lost the biggest account in the territory – a clear case of racial prejudice.

I went in with him and he solved a technical problem for this account. Then I did an illegal thing: I quoted half-price on a tool for this customer. You're supposed to quote the same price to equal customers, unless there's a cost differential to justify a difference. My strategy in quoting half-price was to smoke out whether we had lost the business at that company for any reason other than racial discrimination. They told us we weren't competitive which was obviously untrue, went to our competitor and paid twice as much for that tool. We proved it was racial discrimination.

The moral of the story is, sometimes it is necessary to do the illegal because it is clearly ethical.

Other companies did stick by Alonzo. One of them was Graft-Pelle, a distributor of hoists, electrostatic sprayers and valves. Universal Woods is still doing business with that company today.

We could have changed Alonzo's work assignment, but we didn't. When he was ostracized, we stuck by him. The distributor in Louisville also stuck by him and made sales calls with him. He sold on his merits, and managed to get an average penetration of the market because he was extremely capable. He could really solve problems and was a very good engineer. He was also the first African-American machinist in Louisville.

Sticking by him was the right thing to do – and good business.

Of course, a good diversity program transcends gender barriers, too. That brings up the story of Multi-Metals.

We acquired several companies during our tenure at Vermont American. One of them was Multi-Metals, acquired for $36,000, in the mid-1950s. That company, now part of Robert Bosch Tool Corp., grew into a $20-million-a-year business. It is still based in Louisville and was probably one of the best acquisitions we ever made.

Multi-Metals is a powder metal operation. The plant is well ventilated, but the work is tough and the employees are filthy by the end of the day. Tungsten carbide is 25 percent heavier than lead so the work is physically demanding. For many, many years no women were employed on the factory floor. I was unhappy about that, but the wages and benefits were such that it just did not make sense.

Then early one spring in the late 1970s, I called the president of Multi-Metals and asked, "Are you going to need temporary replacements for vacationers this summer?"

"Yes," he replied.

"Are you going to give preference to students related to employees as usual?"

"Yes."

"OK, one of them is going to be our daughter!"

You could have cut the silence with a knife. But two other women had already been hired by the time our daughter, Margie, arrived to work.

Flashback: Ahead of our time on diversity

"There's only one way to do business, and that's the right way. That kind of thinking really permeated Vermont American more than anything else did. The company was proactive in searching for minorities, when it wasn't very commonplace. We had a couple of women general managers as well as black general managers. There had to be a process over time to get things changed and we changed them. There was consistency all the way across the board."

— *Tim Shea*
Vice President of Finance and
later President
Vermont American

Integrating Louisville's private clubs

Since I joined the Quakers, I have devoted my life trying to do what's right on the job and off. But sometimes that brings me into conflict with others. Sometimes my actions made me a thorn in the side of the ruling establishment in Louisville.

In the late 1950s, a black African from South Africa spoke to our Louisville Friends Meeting (Quakers) about the oppression of apartheid in his country. While he was in Louisville, he was denied service at the coffee shop in the downtown YMCA.

I went to the YMCA director and raised all kinds of hell. He reacted unsympathetically: he told me to take my membership to the all-black Chestnut Street YMCA. So I went to Arthur Kling, a Jewish businessman, and told him my story. Arthur ended up sponsoring me as the first gentile of Louisville's Jewish Community Center.

One good turn deserves another: Arthur and I then sponsored Charlie Richardson as the first black member of the center.

In 1972, I was a member of the Pendennis Club, made up of the city's movers and shakers in business and politics. The trouble was, all of them were white and Christian. Any attempt to bring a black or a Jew into membership was routinely rebuffed, and it took only one member's objection to make it stick. Quakerism teaches equality among all of God's children, no matter what their religion or color. That principle extended to privately owned and run clubs. Some of us at the Pendennis Club set out to change things.

Barry Bingham Jr., then editor of Louisville's *Courier-Journal* newspaper, tried to sponsor department store owner

Dann Byck as a member. The Pendennis membership turned him down flat simply because Dann is Jewish.

Bingham, Maury Johnson, the CEO of the old Citizens Bank and Trust Co., and I quit the Pendennis Club and formed the Jefferson Club that was opened on the top of the just-opened Citizens Bank building. We put on the board of directors Woody Porter, an African-American funeral home director; Sam Greenebaum, a Jewish attorney; and Lewis Hirsch, the Jewish CEO of Paramount Foods.

After the Pendennis/Jefferson Club incident, I got a probably well-deserved reputation as a troublemaker. Consequently, private clubs around town avoided me like the plague. Maury Johnson tried to sponsor me as a member of the Louisville Boat Club, but I was blackballed. They were afraid I'd bring in black guests to play tennis.

Of course, they were right.

Soon I would get my chance, but not at the Louisville Boat Club. The showdown came around 1972 at Standard Country Club, whose membership was all Jewish. Jack Shapero and Ronnie Abrams, two Jewish businessmen in Louisville, sponsored me, but I was blackballed there, too, until a conscientious physician, Dr. "Bubby" Ortner, drew a line in the sand.

I'm told Dr. Ortner called a meeting of the board and told them that he knew my wife, Joan, whom he had had as a student at the University of Louisville School of Medicine. He vouched for me, and said he would resign unless the board capitulated. The board caved in and I became the first gentile member of the club. Early on I brought in members of the Charlie Richardson family, African-Americans, to play tennis at the club.

My efforts to break down racial barriers in Louisville

were not universally embraced. Maury Johnson nominated me for the board of Citizens Fidelity Bank, but I was turned down due to my racial views. I paid a price, but was glad to do so.

Lincoln Foundation

I feel strongly about providing equal opportunities for young people, especially those who are facing poverty or economic disadvantage. The Lincoln Foundation of Louisville is one such organization dedicated to helping disadvantaged youth who need a boost. I've supported it for nearly 50 years.

I was the foundation chairman, and Mansir Tydings was executive director. Several members of the board were part of Moral Rearmament, an international evangelical group that held the patronizing attitude, "We need to do something for the poor blacks."

I was not a founding board member of the Lincoln Foundation. The organization had started many years before I became involved. I became chairman in the late 1950s, when we shifted from a philosophy of white folks doing for poor blacks to "we're in this thing together." We felt that black folks could just as well help disadvantaged whites. Many on the board saw this as heresy. Over the past four decades, the foundation has insisted that all its programs will serve the disadvantaged, no matter what the color of their skin. Also, the board must be diversified. Whites and blacks have held the chair. This is definitely one outfit in town that doesn't know anything about color. The camaraderie is wonderful. We're all friends.

Mansir wanted to change the focus to people working with people, and take religion out of the mix. I backed

Backstory: Moral Rearmament

Moral Rearmament was an international movement founded as the Oxford Group by Frank N. D. Buchman, an American Lutheran minister and evangelist of Swiss descent, and a group of Oxford students in the 1920s. In the late 1930s, as European nations re-armed for war, Buchman called for "moral and spiritual re-armament" as the way to build a "hate-free, fear-free, greed-free world." The Campaign for Moral Re-Armament was launched in 1938. The movement had Christian roots and spawned such programs as "Up With People" during the 1960s and 1970s. It is based around what it calls "The Four Absolutes" – honesty, purity, unselfishness, and love. It became clear at the start of the new millennium that the words "moral re-armament" were no longer appropriate in today's world, and in 2001 the movement adopted the new name of Initiatives of Change.

Mansir. But this proposal ran counter to two board members' vision for the foundation. They threatened to sue me, alleging that I misappropriated the endowment of the foundation, which came from the old Lincoln School. Of course, that was hogwash.

Then a strange thing happened. One of these board members died suddenly. I guess the other member saw this as divine intervention! He quickly dropped the idea of filing suit.

Mansir Tydings was a genius and a man of principle. He was fearless in standing up for what he believed. One day he took an African-American to his Presbyterian church in Anchorage. Church members were mortified, and Mansir really caught the devil. He even had crosses burned on his lawn at his home in upscale Anchorage, Kentucky. So I invited him to attend our Friends' Meeting and he became a pillar of our Meeting.

Mansir did what he did as a dedication of service. He had enough money that he didn't have to worry about how much he was earning. He had the smarts to be the CEO of the old Liberty Bank of Louisville. His family possessed a significant ownership in the bank and he could have carved out a career there – and I believe he would have been very successful and earned a lot more money doing that. But he chose instead to be the business manager of the Lincoln School, helping young people get an education and otherwise move up in society. I'm not sure he ever understood that you could accomplish a lot of the same objectives in the private sector. When the Lincoln School was taken over by the state, he became executive director of the Lincoln Foundation.

One current project of the Lincoln Foundation is to

take a group of seventh or eighth graders and shepherd them through high school with enrichment programs on weekends and in summertime to give them a leg up. If they finish the program, they are guaranteed a college education. The foundation doesn't pay for it. It uses established scholarship programs at participating schools that include Bellarmine University, University of Louisville, Murray State University and Centre College in Kentucky.

Chapter 8 **Accountability**

Good governance in corporations

Too many corporations today have boards that are not truly independent. This was an issue at the Vermont American trial in Chicago (see Chapter 10: Transition).

An arbitrageur, Bob Denison, had bought 100,000 shares of Vermont American stock at $19 a share, giving him a sizable block of stock. Our philosophies could not have been any farther apart. Bob's main business is to get in and out of a company quickly, to make a fast profit on the sale of stock. I have an ethical problem with that. Investors should be in it for the long run, in my opinion. So Bob and I had a lot of differences.

Was he acting unethically? I have a problem with using investments as a source of gambling. But in his case he knew what he was doing and he was making good money at it. The ethical picture gets fuzzy. As I said before, I don't propose to know God's will for other people.

Bob asked me tough questions and made life difficult for me as CEO. I always had to answer to this guy as a major stockholder. So I figured if you can't fight 'em, join 'em, and I encouraged him to come on the board.

You want people to challenge you on your board. As is often said, "If two people agree all the time, one of them is unnecessary." You want independent voices. That makes the company better. Only an executive that is self-confident will take that attitude. If you're timid or worried about keeping your job, you don't usually hold that attitude. You have to respect people's integrity, but you don't have to always agree with them. The people who challenge you are your best friends. They keep you from making mistakes. It's terribly important to have people challenge you. And that includes people who serve on your corporate board.

Flashback: Building consensus on the board and off

"The Vermont American board really sought consensus. Lee controlled the company in the sense that the family had enough votes to vote anybody on or off the board if they wanted. But he had these independent people on the board to help. But the board knew very well that one of the things we should never do is micro-manage. We weren't part of the executive nor did we report to the executive. We were board members, and that's a very different role."

— Bob McDermott
Managing Partner, McDermott Will and Emery
Director of Vermont American
Advisory Board Member of Universal Woods

My mentor, Wight Bakke, was also on our board. He had been training labor leaders on the Yale campus since the 1930s. With Bob Denison, I brought somebody in who had a different point of view than mine.

I try to be accessible to any and all. I have my private phone line printed on my business card. You call me if you've got a problem. I want to know it. I pass out my cards to customers, and at Vermont American that private number was posted in factories all over the world. If you call our switchboard, they're under orders never to ask who it is, and to plug you in to the person you're calling. It's always more fun if a whistle blower calls you rather than calling the newspaper.

Flashback: Pioneer in internal auditing

"Vermont American was definitely a pioneer in the process of an internal audit. Back then it was a little unusual in corporate America for things included in an internal audit to be dealt with at a board level. One of the worst sins you could have committed would have been to hide or attempt to hide a mistake. Lee's integrity and expectations set the tone for the way the company was run."

— *Rob Sage*
Internal Audit Manager and then General Manager
Vermont American's Toccoa Plant

Holistic auditing and worker empowerment

Few companies today perform holistic audits. We were doing them at Vermont American in the 1970s.

A holistic audit is an examination of a business that explores all of the information issues within the organization and in its interactions with its immediate operating environment. This type of audit goes much further than simply looking at a business' financial records. A holistic audit is different from a traditional audit in that it collects and analyzes not only quantitative but also qualitative information, helping to build up a clearer picture of the key issues as well as some of the solutions of potential problems in a business.

In a holistic audit, I get to see the total picture of how a division is being managed. Sure, I'm interested in the financial picture. But I also want to know how receivables are being collected. Are we working with customers as partners in order to get the money in, or are we just chewing on them? I want to know about inventory turns because that is a part of the planning process in business. I want to know about returns and allowances because that tells me something about quality. I want to know about their manifest system on the disposition of toxic material, but I also want to know about what they're doing to reduce the toxic materials that they are using. I want to know about worker empowerment. I want to know about diversity. These are the kinds of things I am interested in finding out. I'm interested in the big picture.

Some ways in which this qualitative data may be collected are:

- Focus groups with different employee groups;
- Questionnaires given to all personnel;
- Walk-through and talk-through assessments during which the business environment is observed and discussed with the employees themselves;
- Feedback from trade unions.

Vermont American had a decentralized management, and

42 people reported to me. True decentralized management is to have so many people report to you that in a sense they report to themselves. I needed to know what was going on. I also needed to be meticulously honest on the validity of the financial statement and the business prospects.

A CEO cannot delegate his or her obligation to know what's going on. He or she has a fiduciary responsibility to the public, to shareholders, to all stakeholders. Vermont American was on the American Stock Exchange. Today, there's a lot of talk about the importance of having a CEO to certify the books and the Securities and Exchange Commission has made a big deal of it. I always assumed that I was responsible for what we were telling the public and that I was responsible for the books at Vermont American. If you're going to know what's going on, you have to work on it. I stood behind all of our public announcements, including the financials.

We had our internal audit department doing holistic audits. Auditors were charged with a very broad list of things they were to investigate. For example, they focused on our environmental performance. They asked the question, "Are we doing the best we can to reduce the amount of toxic material in our plants?"

Our holistic audits were composed of, among other things, the following:

- Division's financial statements;
- Collection of receivables;
- Turnover of inventory;
- Product quality and product safety;
- Shop issues — safety, empowerment and morale;
- Environmental performance;

• Issues that might lead to class-action lawsuits, such as racial discrimination and sexual harassment reports.

At Vermont American, employee empowerment became an issue. When we'd do an audit, we'd look at the issue. I would sit down and talk with the managers. This would give me a chance to shake hands with the people in the shop, get a feel for what was going on, and go out to lunch with the manager. These audits were time-consuming, some taking weeks to complete.

At the conclusion of the audit, a report would be made to the manager and I would discuss it. The bigger divisions were audited every year, the smaller ones every three years.

In addition, I went to trade shows, where you get a chance to see what your competition is doing, and visit with a lot of customers. I guarantee you, if something isn't right, your customer is not at all timid about telling you about it. I also made sales calls right along with our salespeople and made reports through channels just as they did. I encouraged board members to do all of this and call me with ideas.

In the financial part of the audit, we were concerned with whether or not we were collecting our receivables in a timely way, and how we went about it. I wanted to be sure that we handled customers' disagreements properly. I wanted to see that we developed partnerships with our customers and suppliers that enabled us to minimize costs through the system. Our policy has been and is now to require mediation and arbitration clauses with all such partners. These are ethical issues as well as cost issues. Litigation can be very costly.

I have heard of incidents where shipments were billed

in the old year even though they were shipped in the new year. We tolerate economic mistakes, but this would be an ethical mistake and the person responsible would be immediately dismissed.

Workplace empowerment is both an ethical and an economic issue. People develop their spirits making decisions. People closest to the action know more about the production process and how to make it more efficient than management. A good CEO allows the employees to develop their capacity to make good decisions. Making it possible is what leadership is all about. The auditor's role is to make sure the system is working.

In management and organizational theory, "empowerment," or worker responsibility, often refers loosely to the process of giving workers greater control in order to better serve both customers and the employer. While worker empowerment has always been highly motivating and extremely efficient, it has been underutilized because, for most executives, their priority is control.

These two different styles of management – worker responsibility and command and control leadership – came into conflict as early as the 1850s during construction in the west of the Central Pacific Railroad. In the east, the worker responsibility concept was little used – it was socially unacceptable for an engineer to ask a front line worker for advice. Out west, however, the Chinese worked in teams of track layers, and full control of the project was in the hands of the front-line work teams. As a result, track laying increased until it reached a record ten miles in one day, a record that still stands today. The Chinese were so efficient that laws were subsequently passed that made it illegal for them to seek jobs or enter into businesses that Americans wanted. For the Americans, control was more important than efficiency.

After World War II, W. Edwards Deming originated the concept of Quality Circles, a system that enables people at the lowest level to make decisions in their areas of responsibility. He had trouble getting clients in the United States, but Japan, struggling after the war, tried his principles. They so improved Japan's profitability that soon General Motors and Ford were trying to learn what happened.

As an example of how worker empowerment works, Universal Woods sometimes sends a production worker to visit a customer when there is a quality issue. Not only does that person have the best knowledge, but also he or she can help develop a partnership with the customer.

Today, savvy executives consider their employees to be an investment. They recognize that new talent and ideas increase efficiency and that expanding their employees' capabilities through workplace empowerment will increase their value. This may be costly up front, but it reduces cost on the backside.

Safety committees are another kind of worker empowerment. You can't expect people to be productive unless they work in a safe environment. At Universal Woods, before the creation of a dynamic safety committee we were having about 20 accidents per year. That improved drastically to no lost time accidents during a two-year period before we had an accident that broke the string. Then the clock started to run again. Overall our record has improved dramatically with the safety committee.

Our workers compensation insurance cost, which covers accidents in the workplace, was 1.5 percent of sales before we bought this business in 1990. It's now .2 percent. The facts speak for themselves.

Environmental performance auditing is more than just looking to be sure the manifest system is in place and that the company is in legal compliance. What kind of work are we doing to design around toxic materials? Are we using the best and safest methods of disposal? Mistakes can be enormously expensive as well as unethical.

At Vermont American, our internal auditors uncovered a number of performance problems. Once we learned of a Swedish sales agent that wanted his check sent to a New York bank to avoid Swedish income taxes. Of course, we didn't do that. A few years afterwards, I got a call from the guy. "Boy, was I lucky you wouldn't put my money into the New York bank account," he told me, "because I got caught when another company wasn't as sensitive as you were. I paid a huge fine, but if you had done it, too, I'd be in jail!" And on and on it goes. In business you will find the ungodly. But fortunately most people are ethical and our internal auditors helped encourage ethical practices.

Companies should have a value system. They should stand for something, do what they think is morally right. Not everyone will agree with the positions you take or share your convictions.

Companies today are under immense pressure to act ethically. In the wake of the corporate scandals starting with Enron and Arthur Andersen, business people have focused a strong spotlight on the importance of operating ethically. But how do they accomplish that? I have four suggestions for companies:

1. Appoint a board of directors that is independent of the CEO.

2. Split the responsibilities of the chairperson and the president. If that's not possible, at least one lead director on the board should have the responsibility to call a meeting to evaluate the CEO's performance at least annually.

3. Rein in corporate greed by paying reasonable compensation to the top brass. I have a big problem when I see a CEO who downsizes his company and still gets a big bonus. When an executive cuts the work force, he or she should do as I did at Vermont American – take a salary cut.

4. Expense stock options. Many companies are not expensing, or listing, stock options on the profit-and-loss statement. This is a travesty. The European Union and the Securities and Exchange Commission will probably demand that eventually. When I evaluate a company to add to my stock portfolio, I look for potential dilution with stock options. Companies should put a value on stock options and expense them. That gives a more realistic picture of their economic health.

Chapter 9 **Stewardship**

Fish kill and the Superfund

Boone, North Carolina, is primarily a tourist area where a lot of folks go to fish. Our company had an operation there, and made a big mistake: we let toxic material leach into a stream that killed every darn fish in it. Unfortunate though they are, these things do happen. So we sat down with the state of North Carolina to figure what to do about it. We were guilty as sin. We finally settled on paying the retail price per pound for every fish that was killed. It was a novel approach.

The spill was clearly an accident, but you should pay for accidents. When you make a mistake, the only thing you can do is stand up and admit it. Take care of it. It's the ethical thing to do.

I always tried to do the best I could to be a good steward of the environment. However, at Vermont American we did wind up responsible for two Superfund sites, and we had a lot of bad experiences with this. I have always believed that good business needs good regulation by the government, and it certainly needs good regulation in environmental matters. However, in recent years most laws regulating business are written in a way to encourage litigation and to provide opportunities for lawyers to make money. Here's the way it happened for us.

Backstory: Superfund

In December 1980, President Jimmy Carter signed into law the Comprehensive Environmental Response, Compensation and Liability Act of 1980 (CERCLA), more commonly known as Superfund. This legislation was passed to primarily deal with cleaning up hazardous waste sites where owners had shirked responsibility, but also allowed injured parties to sue in federal court for damages.

A Superfund site is any land in the United States that has been contaminated by hazardous waste and identified by the Environmental Protection Agency (EPA) as a candidate for cleanup because it poses a risk to human health and/or the environment. The chemicals found at Superfund sites range from familiar contaminants, like arsenic, lead, mercury, and DDT to less familiar chemicals such as toluene, trichloroethylene, and pentachlorophenol.

One of EPA's top priorities is to get those responsible for the contamination to clean up the site. If the a responsible party be found, is not viable, or refuses to cooperate, EPA, the state, or a Native American tribe may clean up the site using Superfund money. EPA may seek to recover the cost of cleanup from those parties that do not cooperate.

In the early 1980s, we asked the state of Vermont what to do with the trichloroethane sludge that was a byproduct of our operation at our Vermont Tap & Die and Northeast Tool plants in Lyndonville, Vermont. We had recycled as much as we could by using a still, and now it was just gook. But it was toxic. They advised us to put it in the Parker Sanitary Landfill in Lyndon, Vt., so we did.

Then people started moving in near the landfill, and the state of Vermont came back to us and said, "You've got to clean it up."

We said, "Hey, wait a minute, you told us to put it up there."

They said, "We can't help it. The law says you've got to clean it up."

We worked with government, not against it. They recommended we pour asphalt over the site, and nature would take care of the problem in a year or so. We wanted to do it. First, we connected three families to safe drinking water so they weren't drinking from the aquifer. It was going to cost us $250,000. But the newspaper got hold of it and the people were up in arms, telling us to get the stuff out of their back yard. I was still with the company when it was made a Superfund site. At that point, the Federal government assumed jurisdiction.

The U.S. Environmental Protection Agency ordered a study. I understand Vermont American paid $5 million for studies, never mind cleaning the darn thing up. It stayed without a cap for years. Eventually, the state of Vermont, the EPA and the other companies put up the money for it. Everyone except Vermont American settled. They finally did put a cap on it, but 20 years too late.

Because of the delay, it was estimated to take 30 years

to clean up the aquifer. They demanded that Vermont American pay $50 million to flush up all the water in the aquifer and clean it. But here's what finally happened. New technology was developed called bioremediation, a process in which living organisms degrade or transform hazardous organic contaminants. What they've been able to do is to line a trench with this material and as the water flows down the trench, it neutralizes the trichloroethylene. So now Bosch has agreed to clean up the landfill and the cost will be a little less than $10 million rather than the original estimate of $50 million.

By the time the company settled with the insurers, I had already left Vermont American. My friends there protected me, telling the insurers not to include me in any litigation. That made me feel wonderful, but I did end up hiring my own counsel. He was Louis M. Rundio Jr., a Chicago attorney specializing in environmental law. As I remember it, his rate was $450 an hour. He worked on another client's case when he was on the plane to see me or when he was not working with me on the deposition. I thought I would get a bill for $25,000 to $30,000, but he billed me for only $2,000. It could have been a lot higher if another, less scrupulous attorney had handled the case. Lou Rundio may be one of the most expensive attorneys around, but he's also one of the most ethical.

What are the ethical issues in the Parker Landfill episode? The EPA approves who will conduct a study of a Superfund site. But there's a huge potential for graft, especially when there are so many studies ordered. Today, at Universal Woods, environmental stewardship is one of our overriding concerns. Many businesses in our industry are polluting the air with volatile organic compounds

(VOCs). We are not, but that doesn't make us perfect in all respects when it comes to the environment. We do have major challenges ahead in the disposal of sawdust and urea-formaldehyde.

The World Health Organization considers formaldehyde as a carcinogen. In Europe it's no longer produced in particleboard and fiberboard where the resin binder is urea-formaldehyde. However, it would be financially impossible for us to substitute some other substance for formaldehyde in our own production. In short, there would be enough of a cost differential to put us out of business.

The main issue is trying to get particleboard and fiberboard that is free of formaldehyde. Our sources have reduced the percentage to under two percent, but we're still asking our board manufacturers what they are doing to find a solution and determine the costs involved. My concern is how urea-formaldehyde affects our customers and our employees. And I'm worried that it could become a litigious issue.

As for sawdust, it would be best to use it for fuel. Unfortunately, it explodes. We've talked about using it in stables, but it's so fine that it gets caught in horses' hooves. We're still trying to come up with a way to properly dispose of it.

Chapter 10 **Transition**

Nothing in life stays the same. That goes for business, too.

By the late 1980s, Vermont American became the target for takeover by corporate raider Newell Corp. of Freeport, Illinois. This was a very stressful time for everyone at our company. Before it was finished, I was out as chairman and the company had changed hands – but not to Newell. And we had written new corporate takeover law known as "the Quaker defense." Here's the story:

Newell began buying up Vermont American stock and the struggle for control ensued. Our company began buying its own stock. I had 26 percent of the voting shares. All but about a half-dozen employees holding stock in the 401(k) pension plan were prepared to vote with me. Then Newell claimed fraud, suing both the company and me. They alleged that I was engaged in a deal to save my own neck. In its lawsuit, Newell was demanding $17 million from me.

In a separate action, a class-action lawsuit claiming fraud was filed against me in Delaware demanding a whole lot more. If that had been successful, my attorney told me I would have been bankrupt.

Newell went to federal court in the summer of 1989 and got an injunction prohibiting Vermont American from buying additional stock. Judge James B. Zagel issued the injunction. Because it was a civil and not a criminal matter, Judge Zagel would not grant me a jury trial. It seemed likely that he had already determined that I was guilty.

When it seemed as if it couldn't get any worse, it did. Within days of the injunction, the second-largest shareholder on the board agreed to sell stock to Newell. That block of stock, combined with the 17 percent that Newell already owned provided them with 42 percent of the company versus my 26 percent and those employees who would vote for me. It wasn't clear at that point how the remaining shareholders would vote.

I knew if Newell got control, the company would be no more. Newell had a history of stripping assets, closing plants and laying off employees.

The sale of the company wasn't good for the employees no matter which way you went. We knew we couldn't save the company, so we opted for the lesser of two evils, a "white knight."

A white knight is a person or company that comes to the rescue of another company that is being threatened by a hostile takeover. The intention of the white knight is to circumvent the takeover of the object of interest by a third, unfriendly entity, which is perceived to be less favorable. The knight might defeat the undesirable entity by offering a higher and more enticing bid, or strike a favorable deal with the management of the object of acquisition.

Our white knight was a partnership between the Bosch Group of Stuttgart, Germany and Emerson Electric Co. of St. Louis. With these two in charge, it seemed the operation would have to be run from Louisville, so we could save the administrative jobs. After 10 years, there was to be a sunset provision where one had to buy the other out. (Bosch bought out Emerson in 2002. Sadly, it announced plans to move the offices to the Chicago area. It also formed Robert Bosch Tool Corp. about that time.)

An agreement was reached to sell the company in August 1989.

The following month, the fraud case was heard in Zagel's court in Chicago. Our fate was squarely in the hands of the federal judge. I was pessimistic. It looked like the game was over. So I took a big block of Vermont American stock and put it into a charitable foundation, which today is worth almost $22 million. I gave a small block of stock to my wife, Joan, which they said I could do. Having a foundation meant we could continue to help not-for-profit organizations. I figured we could both live off what Joan had and our standard of living wouldn't suffer appreciably.

But the worst-case scenario I kept imagining didn't happen.

The judge asked me to raise my hand and swear to tell the truth. Quakers do not take such an oath. I said, "Look, I don't swear. I tell the same story on the street corner that I do in this court, and I'm perfectly happy to be bound by the rules of perjury either place." The judge replied, "That's good enough for me." I was willing to stand on principle, and I think that helped my case.

I testified on my own behalf, and I talked about why the company board minutes had not recorded any negative votes. It was because we handled our board meetings like a Quaker business meeting: we tried to reach consensus. There were occasions when somebody wasn't totally convinced. Gene Cowley didn't like us having a company airplane, for instance. But he said if we didn't use it for

Backstory: Quakers and Oath-Taking

Quakers believe that truth is vital in all dealings of life. They regard the custom of taking oaths as not only contrary to the teachings of Jesus, (principally based on the words of Jesus in the Sermon on the Mount: "I say to you: 'Swear not at all'" [Matthew 5:34]) but as setting a double standard of truthfulness. Quakers, instead, simply affirm that they will tell the truth, emphasizing that their statement is only a part of their usual integrity of speech.

Opposition to oath-taking caused many problems for Quakers throughout their history. They were frequently imprisoned because of their refusal to swear loyalty oaths. Testifying in court was also difficult. George Fox, the founder of Quakerism, famously challenged a judge who had asked him to swear, saying that he would do so once the judge could point to any Bible passage where Jesus or his apostles took oaths. Legal reforms from the eighteenth century onwards now allow everyone in the United Kingdom the right to make an affirmation instead of an oath. The United States has permitted affirmations since it was founded and they are even mentioned in the Constitution.

personal reasons, he wouldn't stand in our way. We didn't vote on the board, and neither do Quakers when they make a decision. Quakers try to reach unity, or consensus, so everybody is on board with a decision. That's how I tried to run the company. The judge found in my favor. Informally, he said, "I was sure glad to be able to come down on the side of the good guys." I got my share of the takeover; otherwise I would have been bankrupt. He said he wasn't sure he would have found the same way had we already sold the company.

The judge took into consideration the fact that the company had already chosen a white knight. He also considered the testimony by the investment banker that there was a huge difference between Vermont American – committed to growth from within the organization, and Newel – which had grown entirely by hostile takeovers. Judge Zagel ruled our takeover defenses were legitimate. He said Newell's takeover would destroy the unique corporate culture of Vermont American, where the board and I ran the company by consensus.

Judge Zagel's ruling made new case law, the so-called "Quaker defense." It's made up of two issues:

The first issue is that when two companies are run very differently, their cultures are not going to be compatible. Therefore, you have a right to make that an issue in a proposed takeover. It may be akin to the stakeholder theory where legitimate stakeholders are owed an obligation by the organization and its leaders. Under Newell, the office in Louisville would have been shut down. We had a right to fight against a hostile takeover.

Second issue: A corporate board sometimes operates on consensus. But you can't make the assumption, that it is not independent from the CEO. The board was not in my pocket. It questioned me and had an independent voice.

Obviously, Newell didn't see it that way. Walter Greenough, Newell's attorney in the federal case, told the *Chicago Tribune* in a 1990 interview, "Newell's success is based on making its acquisitions more profitable. It kicks management in the butt and gets them moving."

But Zagel cast Newell in a more negative light, saying, "In order to generate increased profitability, Newell at times would follow its acquisitions by asset-stripping, plant closures and layoffs."

The only real defense I know of against a hostile takeover involves super voting stock for insiders. That is why Louisville-based Brown-Forman Corp., one of the largest American-owned companies in the wine and spirits business, is still independent. The use of super voting stock is an anti-takeover defense plan implemented by issuing a dividend of preferred stock with voting rights. In this strategy, if an investor acquires a substantial block of a firm's voting stock, preferred holders (other than the large block holder) become entitled to super voting privileges. Hence, it is difficult for the block holder to obtain voting control.

But you have to institute the super voting stock when you first go public; otherwise it is unethical and probably illegal. I wish I had done it, but I didn't have the foresight.

Coincidentally, I was teaching ethics at Wilmington College, a Quaker school in Ohio, in 2003 when I bumped into a former Newell executive who was also teaching there. He said he quit the company when they demanded he dismantle a company they had acquired. "It didn't pass the mother test, so I quit," he said. (The mother test is a test by which a decision can be determined ethical or unethical:

if you can't tell your mother about it, you'd better not be doing it.)

Newell did not get to take over Vermont American, but they made over 100 percent on their investment. Sometimes the ungodly wins. But in the end, we successfully kicked Newell in the butt and got it moving – out of the picture.

Flashback: Open communication

"If I were a drill operator working at the plant in Greenville, N.C. or anywhere else, and wanted to speak to the president of the company, I could talk to him. At Vermont American you had that right, and that was pretty terrific."

— George Chapman
General Manager and Vice President of Manufacturing
American Saw & Tool

Newell and Thomas Industries

At the same time Newell was buying stock from Vermont American, it also took aim at Thomas Industries Inc., a Louisville company started by my dad. They figured both were "sleeping beauties," the term used for companies ripe for takeover. They started to make their move in 1986 after my father died.

After Newell bought a chunk of Thomas Industries' stock, the executives there thought they were about to be taken over, too. As it turned out, Newell wanted only Thomas' Paint Applicator division to combine with EZ

Paintr, their manufacturer of paint rollers, which they also owned. They wanted to achieve economies of scale.

Newell ended up selling Paint Applicator for the Newell stock and a standstill agreement in which Newell ceased buying Thomas Industries' stock. At the Vermont American trial, Newell president Dan Ferguson bragged what a great deal they had orchestrated with Thomas Industries. Paint Applicator was worth much, much more than what the stock was worth. In essence, it's called "green mail." I think it's unethical because other stockholders cannot get more than the going price for their stock. They're the losers.

Greenmail or greenmailing is a corporate acquisition strategy for generating large amounts of money from an attempted hostile takeover of a company. This tactic is an adaptation of the corporate raid strategy of taking over an undervalued company, dismembering it, and selling off its valuable pieces for a profit. Once having secured a large share of a target company, instead of completing the hostile takeover, the greenmailer offers instead to end the threat to the victim company by selling his share back to it – at a vastly inflated price.

If you honestly valued Paint Applicator and the stock that Newell owned, it probably would have had to put in another $25 million in the deal to be fair to the other shareholders.

Thomas Industries also bought a lighting-fixture company from Emerson Electric Co. for far more than it was worth and borrowed a huge sum of money to do it. This reduced the value of Thomas Industries to the point that nobody would want to buy the company. This is called the "scorched-earth defense" against possible takeovers.

The scorched-earth defense is another form of anti-takeover strategy whereby the target firm makes itself unattractive to the hostile bidder by liquidating or destroying all valuable assets, scheduling debt repayment to be due immediately following the hostile takeover, and so on.

Saving the independence of a local company is an ethical thing to do. It saves jobs and helps the local economy. You have a tradeoff here. I do not think it is proper to trash the shareholders to accomplish that. That is why we chose an alternative to Newell that would save a larger percentage of the jobs.

I saw how Thomas Industries was being managed even before all of this happened with Newell. I tried unsuccessfully to get the CEO replaced with Tim Brown. When that failed, I realized I could no longer continue on the board in good conscience. (Remember the Jacuzzi story in Chapter 1?) I had the choice of resigning or taking them to court. I don't take people to court, so I resigned and gave my small block of stock to Bellarmine University in Louisville. I got a tax deduction of just under $25 a share. It took Thomas Industries 10 years of a roaring bull market before its stock got back to that level.

I tried to stand on principle: You have responsibilities to the other shareholders and your employees. That's why I wouldn't pay greenmail to Newell. I wasn't going to sell part of the company and make a bad deal. If I had caved into Newell's greenmail overture, I would have been guilty of what they sued me for.

Tim Brown eventually became the CEO and ran the company ethically and competently until it was sold to Garner Denver in 2005.

Chapter 11 **Partnerships**

Buying Universal Woods

By 1990, I was walking the streets. Business had been my life, and it was only a matter of time before I would land on my feet again. I discovered a business for sale in the Bluegrass Industrial Park in Jeffersontown, Kentucky, a Louisville suburb. As it had been at Vermont American, my goal at Universal Woods was to build an ethical business. But there were many challenges.

Paul Neumann was still at Vermont American. A fellow Quaker, he has unquestionably strong business ethics. When I discovered the owner had a health problem and could no longer work with me, I was worried. Then out of the blue Paul called. He wanted to come to work with me. But he was on a track to become the next chief operating officer of Vermont American and coming to work with me meant he was laying his financial security on the line.

"You're nuts," I told him. "I don't care, I want to go to work with you," he replied. Within weeks, he was on board at Universal Woods. Paul Wilson also came over from Vermont American. Terry Newhouse and Jim Woodhouse, who had worked at Vermont American, joined me as well. They all wanted to work in the old-style corporate culture where ethics count.

How lucky can you get? Paul Neumann is probably

the best business executive I've ever worked with. He has more imagination about partnerships than I ever had. He's better at marketing, and picked up the technology very quickly.

Paul and his partnerships

Our little company employs fewer than 50 people, but our reach is international and that's due to our network of partnerships. Partnerships don't mean maximizing profit at any price. Before we strike a partnership with an overseas company, we make sure they measure up to high standards of working conditions and worker treatment.

Paul arranged a partnership with a competitor, Rowmark. Rowmark is a leader in the engraving business and we do UNISUB™ for sublimated products. Instead of fighting it out, we developed a partnership with them. We sold them the private label UNISUB™ under a different name for the U.S. only. Internationally, we have a joint venture. UNISUB™ is sold under our brand and their brand, so there's a broader product line and we get the distributors. So we have a distributors' network around the world. Forming that network on our own would have been a huge expense. So we saved money and got a good partnership in the bargain.

One of Rowmark's distributors, from Bombay, India, visited us at Universal Woods recently. When he came in, I showed him the picture that has been hanging on my wall for 40 years – Gandhi's. He took out his note pad. It had Gandhi's picture on the cover. That opened up an instant line of communication between us. His visit gave us an opportunity to improve relationships between our countries. Our company is too small to do anything big.

But in a tiny way we're making our contribution to world peace.

One caveat: You can't get together with a direct competitor. That would run you afoul of ethics and the law. You cannot connive with competitors against customers. But in the case with Rowmark, they make engraving and we make sublimation. It's very different.

Sometimes partnerships can get a little too cozy. When I was with Vermont American we had a wonderful relationship with Sharon Steel Corp. in Pennsylvania. We were working with them to develop additives in steel to make the ideal saw blade. One Christmas, they sent me a very expensive silver tray as a present. But the silver tray was in marked contrast to the can of maple syrup from Vermont that we sent all our suppliers.

They probably weren't trying to buy me. It was more than likely a gesture of good will. But something about the silver tray just didn't smell right. Our company slogan was, "If it doesn't smell right, then don't do it!"

We sent the silver tray back.

Unfortunately, the family that owned the lion's share of Sharon Steel also lost a hostile takeover fight. It did not go to a white knight, and a nogoodnik ended up getting them. A corporate raider destroyed that company and it ended up going out of business. Nothing is forever.

My dad and Gene Cowley invited people from Sears to attend the Kentucky Derby. But the Sears people paid their own airfare and their own hotel bill. They took the Vermont American people out to breakfast. Then Dad provided the Derby tickets and hosted a party. I didn't go to the Derby.

You need to have a relationship with your supplier or

customer. It's important to go out and break bread. It's important to maintain a friendship. But at the same time, you have to be very careful to keep gifts small in value. We tried to build a relationship built on quality, service and price, and not on who showed up with the best hams at Christmas.

Flashback: Lessons learned at Vermont American

"Success can come without deception or mistreating others;

Modesty is the best policy;

Concern and care for others will pay dividends— personally and financially— but it better be genuine;

Be open to criticism, even from people who work with you;

Speak your mind when appropriate."

—George Chapman
General Manager and Vice President of Manufacturing
American Saw & Tool

Compulsory arbitration

As a Quaker, I believe in building cooperative relationships – in all aspects of life, including our business. So when it comes to signing contracts, Vermont American always put in this provision: If there is a disagreement and we can't solve the issue, we must turn over the matter to binding arbitration.

Binding arbitration is a negotiation in which both parties in a dispute agree to accept an impartial observer's resolution of the dispute. It is a form of alternative dispute resolution (ADR) and is a legal alternative to litigation. Many believe that the present lawyer-oriented litigation system does not work in the vast majority of cases. The cost of defense alone often places the defendant or his insurance carrier in a no-win position as well. ADR methods such as binding arbitration were therefore designed to streamline the judicial process. Benefits of binding arbitration include savings of time and money, a lesser degree of animosity between the parties than one finds in the court setting, developing solutions that better fit the best interests of the parties, possible preservation of business relationships, and the option of compromise, as distinguished from the "winner take all" philosophy which often prevails in the litigation setting.

The same holds true at Universal Woods. We never sign a contract without a compulsory arbitration clause. We have such a clause on the back of our invoice and one on our acknowledgement.

Paul Neumann negotiated a joint venture with Rowmark that includes the following clause:

"Any disputes arising from the joint relationship that cannot be resolved between the two parties shall first be addressed with mediation. If these issues cannot be resolved with mediation, they will then be submitted to binding arbitration without the presence of attorneys. It is agreed that the two parties will meet on a quarterly basis to review performance and progress of this agreement."

We trust each other, but we still meet quarterly with Rowmark to keep open the lines of communication. If a problem comes up, we would go into mediation. Failing that, we would go to binding arbitration. You don't want lawyers involved because they tend to be contentious. If there's a problem, you want an arbitrator to keep these partnerships strong.

Once a representative of the holding company that had sold us Universal Woods gave us notice they were filing suit. A dispute arose between us on who was responsible for paying a health care bill for one of our employees. The employee had been hurt when they owned the company and they were trying to stick us with the bill. I guess they figured that with their deep pockets they could cause us to spend so much money that we would be forced to settle. Our attorney just laughed at them because we had a compulsory arbitration clause in the sale contract. "Look at your contract," he told them. That was the last we heard from them. Lawyers don't like me at all!

One former colleague of mine has a little business and he billed somebody $2,000, and the customer said the product was no good. He never returned it and didn't pay up, daring my friend to sue. You can't sue for $2,000. But if you have an arbitration clause in place, your chances of recouping your money are better. So I guarantee you, today he has a compulsory arbitration clause on all of his invoices. He learned an expensive lesson.

In business today there is a significant trend away from adversarial relationships between customers and suppliers. Partnerships make for a much more profitable relationship as well as being a lot more fun. All contracts entered into by Universal Woods have a compulsory arbitration clause that includes a prohibition against going to court.

I believe that it is contrary to the basic tenets of our Religious Society of Friends (Quakers) to take people to court over a civil disagreement. George Fox founded the

Society about 1650, long before our current litigious patterns developed. Fox said, "Away with those lawyers, twenty shilling Counselors, thirty shilling Sergents, ten groat Attorneys, that will throw men into prison for a thing of naught."

The early Friends had a Testimony against taking people to court. Today, I believe that's still valid. Fox had it right.

Setting up SA8000

Nearly everybody has heard of ISO 9000. ISO 9000 is a management structure, but there are no absolute standards. You set your own goals and seek continuous improvement. However, there are absolute standards for SA8000, which I was privileged to help develop through the Council on Economic Priorities.

The term ISO (International Organization for Standardization) 9000 refers to a set of quality management standards. ISO first published these quality standards in 1987, revised them in 1994, and then republished an updated version in 2000. ISO's purpose is not to dictate how to make well-made products or supply superior service. Rather, IS0 9000 was designed to facilitate international trade by providing a single set of standards that people everywhere would recognize and respect. These standards include such aspects as how a business selects its suppliers, what checks are made on both incoming and outgoing goods, how a company makes sure its staff is trained to do its jobs, and how the company improves its systems.

SA8000 is a voluntary, universal standard for companies interested in auditing and certifying labor practices in their facilities and those of their suppliers and vendors. It was developed by Social Accountability International (SAI), known until recently as the Council on Economic Priorities Accreditation Agency. SAI is a non-profit affiliate of the Council on Economic Priorities (CEP). This standard is based on international workplace norms in the International Labour Organization conventions (a division of the United Nations) and the UN's Universal Declaration of Human Rights and the Convention on Rights of the Child. It is a way for businesses to maintain just and decent working conditions throughout their supply chains. This comprehensive standard includes sections on child and forced labor, health and safety, freedom of association and right to collective bargaining, discrimination, discipline, working hours, compensation and management systems.

The "SA" in SA8000 stands for social accountability. This voluntary standard was developed in 1996 based on the International Labour Organization (ILO) and other human rights conventions.

We don't want to get stuck with the sweatshop label. SA8000 is the global standard for workplace issues such as living wage, basic worker safety, gender equality, no children under 14-years-of-age on the payroll, the formation of a funeral association, etc. And it's audited by one of the international-auditing firms.

The not-for-profit Council on Economic Priorities was concerned with the peace testimony, the Defense Department budget, and ethical investing. These are three issues that I've been passionate about all my adult life. SA8000 became an overriding passion for the council, which spawned the unique organization Social Accountability International. And although the council is now defunct, Social Accountability International is alive and well and continues to certify auditors to audit SA8000 companies.

Much has been written in the media lately about Enron, WorldCom, Global Crossings and other companies accused of malfeasance. Business executives from these companies are giving everybody a black eye. But there are ethical businesses out there. For example, Avon is insisting all their sources become certified SA8000, so they're not doing business with any sweatshops. Toys "R" Us and Dole are doing the same thing.

SA8000 does not require immediate compliance and wouldn't succeed if it did. But it does require a company to make continuous, meaningful progress toward the established standards. One extremely important standard is a living wage, which is calculated to ensure a worker can afford to pay for good nutrition based on a diet of 2,200 calories per day. The standards also call for a worker to have the freedom to join a union. But in China unions are illegal. Gender discrimination is condemned under SA8000, but how quickly can it be a force for change in the Islamic world where such discrimination is widespread? Nothing is perfect.

To be certified, a company must have a certification audit by an auditor judged to be independent by Social Accountability International. Most of us do not like to be subjected to demands and criticism. SA8000's certification process may make more than a few companies uncomfortable, if not downright defensive. But in the wake of Enron and all of the other corporate scandals, there is a huge demand for transparency. That transparency runs across the board from financial reporting to disclosures on how business treats its employees. This is a healthy process for world business.

SA8000 does not provide a panacea for all of the injustices. But it is a growing movement and as of this writing 710 factories in 45 countries have been certified as compliant. (For more information online, visit http://www.cepaa.org/SA8000/SA8000.htm)

Flashback: Open to criticism

"One of the best things about Lee Thomas was that he was totally open to criticism. You could go in to see him and be very upset, saying he's doing everything wrong. He would just sit there and listen until you were through. At that time he would tell you what he thought and he never swore when he spoke. That is why I worked for him and why I came back to work after leaving. He was one of the few people who really lived that creed: 'I'm going to listen to the people who work with me. When there are major decisions I want to hear both sides of the argument not just what I think is the right way to go.'"

— George Chapman
General Manager and Vice President of Manufacturing
American Saw & Tool

Chapter 12 **Globalization**

The CEO as World Citizen

Companies today need to be citizens of the world. We need to use our economic might constructively. If we do that we can increase the prosperity of our companies and also help the cause of world peace. During my business career, I have made it a point to do a lot of international traveling, getting acquainted with people, trying to figure out how to make our businesses more international. The fact is, people are people. We're all God's children – no matter where we live.

In my extensive travels, I encountered some awful working conditions, and refused to do business with those who were mistreating or neglecting their workers. But I also met a lot of conscientious people along the way. When it comes to ethics in the global marketplace, it's a mixed bag.

My goal in business has always been to strive to be a world-class player. But if you're going to be in business today, you've got to understand the world. That's the objective. Of course, you don't always see a pretty picture.

My Armenian friend

Even when governments are at odds, individuals can still forge friendships.

During a 1960 Moscow trip, I went to the huge Gum department store to find a chess set for our son Glenn. I was having a terrible time because I didn't speak Russian. But fate intervened in the form of a perfect stranger, Shahen Hamandjian, who took me in hand and got me my chess set.

Then we went to lunch. I reached for the check but he chastised me playfully and took it – and a lifelong friendship was born.

In 1970, I took my wife, Joan, to Moscow and then to Armenia to meet Shahen and his wife, Emma. We went to their home and had a party, and got into discussions. Both he and his wife were English professors. I wanted to talk about Czechoslovakia, which had been recently invaded by the Soviets, and he wanted to talk about Vietnam.

In 1980, he came to the U.S. to visit his daughter, who by this time had immigrated to Los Angeles, and he stayed in our home. We had quite a party. He died about three years ago.

Poking fun in Japan

In the late 1960s, I was riding a train in Europe when I met Judge Shinzeki of Japan. Later when I was on business in Tokyo, I called the judge's home and a woman answered the phone. I told her that I wanted the whole family to come down to the Imperial Hotel and have dinner with me, Western-style. She gave me the judge's office number and I called him. He said, "My son and I would be delighted to have dinner with you, but the women are indisposed." I hadn't been talking to his wife earlier. It was actually his daughter, and she had a full head of steam to have dinner with this crazy American! Later the judge, having learned about my conversation with his daughter, called me and, laughing, said, "Well, Lee, I guess we'll have to do this your way."

At the dinner, his wife brought me the loveliest hand-made Geisha doll, which we still have in our living room today, and we were having a really good time. We had no sooner sat down than Judge Shinzeki bounced up and ran halfway across the room. He bowed down to his kneecaps, then came back laughing. He had met up with the justices of the Japanese Supreme Court who remarked they had not seen a party like this in all of their lives. It was very unusual in those days in Japan to see men and women dining together.

The Shinzekis called me "Thomas-san" or Mr. Thomas. But I told them, "Why don't you call me by my Japanese name, "Tomago?" That's the Japanese word for egg, and the name had been given to me by the Japanese who were working on my base after World War II because I was an "egghead," working with books. I gave it another meaning, too: bald. I was making fun of the fact that I didn't have much hair. I guess it's safer and wiser to poke fun at yourself rather than at others. (Our daughter Margie tells me that "Tomago" also means white on the outside and yellow on the inside. I'll accept that.)

We continued our friendship for more than 30 years. After Judge Shinzeki died, his daughter contacted me, remembering me by Tomago, my Japanese name.

Nazi drama in Finland

Vermont American had a supplier in Finland making hand tools, mostly files and rasps. One time I took my family there. We had an eye-opening experience at an outdoor drama about World War II.

Believe it or not, the heroes of this drama were the Nazis. Most of the world detested the Nazis, and for good reason. But during the war Finland had invited the Nazis into the country to help contend against the Russians. The Finns had a long history of conflict with the Russians. The Nazis let the Finns run their own affairs and did not impose Nazism.

So in this drama, the Nazis were the heroes. We had a fascinating conversation that day with our Finnish hosts. Incidentally, both of us held similar views on the evils of Nazism.

Lessons learned in China

After President Nixon opened up China for cultural and business exchanges, Joan made the trip with her college alumni friends. I came to scout around for possible sources of tools. Quakers were welcome in China because they had provided aid during that country's terrible civil war. Joan and I visited the Hall of the People, the Great Wall and Forbidden City. It was wonderful and the hospitality was great.

Actually, Joan had arrived in China a couple of weeks ahead of me. Out of the goodness of their hearts, the Chinese rearranged schedules so she and I could visit the major tourist attractions together. After that, she went on her tour with fellow alumni of Swarthmore College, and I visited factories.

Some of the sights weren't so pleasant.

In Nanking, I saw a factory that was absolutely deplorable. The dust in the grinding room was so thick that you could hardly see. Silicosis had been discovered at the turn of the 20th century, so the plant's operators should have known breathing this dust could cause terrible consequences for the workers. In fact, silicosis still kills thousands of people every year, according to a 2000 report from the World Health Organization. Nevertheless, the workers were breathing the silica dust in this grinding room. There were no safeguards employed there. This was not only unhealthful; it was appalling.

Then I witnessed a woman holding a chisel and a guy hitting the head of that chisel with a sledgehammer. She had no protection for her hands. How long would it be before he missed? It was just dreadful. I told my host there was no way I could do business with this factory. The trip to China was falling apart.

But soon it would get even worse.

At dinner with my Chinese hosts, I opened my big mouth and started talking about war. I told them that all war is wrong, whether you're talking about "our" war in Vietnam or "your" war in Tibet.

Here I was, an American, a guest in their country, making an extreme statement that was far from conciliatory. It was a big-time mistake. All hell broke loose. They took great offense. Everybody was shouting at once. I was afraid for my safety and I'm lucky I wasn't arrested. Everybody finally calmed down and we ate our dinner, but I didn't make any friends that day.

The moral: You've got to prepare the way carefully before you can talk about things that are controversial. It is terribly important to have sensitivity to different cultures.

Today, there are SA8000 companies in China. Those companies are making rapid progress toward achieving a living wage and taking a stand against child labor. However, labor unions are still illegal in China and non-government organizations are very closely controlled.

How do you accomplish some kind of protection for workers against despotism? The best you can do in China is to require they have a panel of employees not part of management that will hear grievances and pass them along to management while safeguarding employees against getting fired for speaking up. They've made progress in individual cases.

Today, all the significant tool companies in the world do business in China. They've made progress in quality and factory conditions. It is one of the fastest growing economies in the world. We continue to look for Chinese business partners.

India: Laughter defuses tension

In the mid-1980s, at the request of the Council on Foreign Relations, I was asked to go on an informal negotiating mission to Calcutta to talk about tensions between India and the U.S. The biggest problem was we were reducing our foreign aid. Also, we were not selling fissionable material for their nuclear power plants. There were also some trade issues. Business people from both countries and quasi-government people attended.

We got on the topic of foreign aid and the decibels in the room started to get very high. Finally, I said, "Wait a minute. We've got a problem because we're in a darn cold war. It's expensive and we can't afford everything. The whole thing reminds me of the fellow who came home from a business trip a day early. He found his wife with another man and he went in the closet and got out his gun and put it to his own head. She said, 'Wait a minute, I can explain everything.' And he said, 'Shut up, you're next!' Well, that's the cold war." They broke out in a laugh, and then we all got down to business.

Moral: Sometimes you need a little humor. It humanizes any discussion, no matter how serious.

India again: Baksheesh or no baksheesh

In the late 1960s, Vermont American made a deal to provide equipment to a small Indian company to make threading tools to sell only in India. We got a small stock interest in the company in exchange. But there was a formidable hurdle: The deal required approval from the government in Calcutta.

It doesn't take very many dollar bills to make a bushel basket of rupees. Baksheesh (bribery) is very common. Historically, it started out as a tip, now it's a bribe. The Indian involved in the company was a disciple of Gandhi. He said, "We don't pay baksheesh. This is a democratic nation. Pressure will build. We will just wait. The pressure will build and we'll get our deal."

It was a long wait, six months, but eventually the deal was approved— without baksheesh!

This story ends on a sour note: Eventually the company had a sit-down strike that went on so long that the company went out of business and we lost our $75,000 investment.

But at least we didn't pay any baksheesh!

UN environmental summit

In 1992, the Quaker United Nations Office had run out of money for the last symposium before the Earth Summit in Rio de Janeiro. The summit's chief business was to help governments reconsider economic development and find ways to stop the destruction of finite natural resources and the pollution of the planet. The symposium was to be held in Mohawk, New York, and draw ambassadors from many countries. The environment is one of my strong interests. I said, "I'll put up the $25,000 if I can go." They said, "Well, OK, but you have to keep your mouth shut." And that's tough for me!

I agreed. As an unofficial observer, I was in for an eye-opening experience.

I heard ambassadors of China, Bolivia and other countries tell the U.S., "Look, you've got your standard of living and you polluted the hell out of the environment to do it. We're going to raise our standard of living and will even pollute if there's no other way." Our ambassador was continually frustrated because Washington wouldn't back him. And our government refused to sign environmental treaties.

I remember an African woman at the symposium talking about the population problem, and urging women to learn all they could about their bodies. Of course, the biggest problem is the population explosion. And the answer to that is increased educational opportunities and raising awareness.

Interestingly, the work at the symposium didn't get done so much in the formal sessions. The real work was done in private on the trails around the lake, where ambassadors went for a walk and talked over the issues.

The Earth Summit attracted nearly 10,000 journalists from around the globe transmitting messages about poverty and affluence and how both affect the environment. The summit influenced all subsequent UN conferences. In

1993, for instance, the World Conference on Human Rights in Vienna emphasized the rights of humanity to a healthy environment and to development.

The interconnectedness of the world

Some countries, such as the United States, act like an 800-pound gorilla when it comes to dealing with the world. That creates nothing but animosities. It's far better to promote the interconnectedness of the world. Or so I've tried to teach our children.

As an Amherst College student, our son, Glenn, spent one summer studying Russian in Leningrad. He also spent two summers programming a German computer for a German company in Germany. He took junior year in high school at a gymnasium (high school) in Germany. He was the only American student. Our other children, Rees and Margie, and our grandson, Steve, did the same thing.

In 1990, Glenn and I took a business trip to Russia on behalf of the Council on Economic Priorities. We toured factories in Leningrad and Moscow that made electronic equipment, rockets, tools and other hardware for the Soviet defense establishment. I was in good hands: Glenn understood all technical matters in the native tongue.

Glenn is fluent in Russian, German and Spanish. Margie is fluent in German, and speaks a little French. Rees is fluent in German and Spanish.

The aim was to get them some cultural experience, learn another language completely, and immerse them in the culture of their host nation.

My family and I have traveled around the world. In the mid-1960s we went into East Berlin after the wall had been erected. We were tourists and we got a chance to visit a Friends Meeting in the Communist-dominated part of the divided city. You've got to try to meet the people where they live to understand their perspective on the world.

In my judgment, the world will function a whole lot better and businesses will function a whole lot better if we work together with people and develop partnerships. That's what I've tried to teach our children.

Conclusion

The late Thomas Merton was a monk at the Abbey of Our Lady of Gethsemane at Trappist, Kentucky. He talks about a revelation when he was standing on the corner of what is now Fourth Street and Muhammad Ali in Louisville. "I was suddenly overwhelmed with the revelation that I loved all these people, that they were mine, and I theirs." He also wrote about the importance of evaluating our actions as they appear to others.

Like so many principles, this is important in our striving for world peace and is also vital in managing a good, profitable business. I hear lots of anti-Muslim prejudice. My Islamic friends are just as concerned about terrorism as I am. But Thomas Merton and I will both be asking how our killing of innocent Muslims in Iraq looks to ordinary Islamic people the world over. Can we ever form partnerships that will help us apprehend the terrorists?

On one occasion many years ago, I was at the kibbutz Hanita on the Lebanese border in Israel. They had a factory making end mills and milling cutters using some of the same German machine tools that we used. We used to compare notes. It was a kind of informal partnership. One time when I was there, the leader of the kibbutz asked me if I would like to go on a mission to negotiate with the Bedouins. Their goats were climbing the fences and getting into the citrus groves of the kibbutz. The government of Israel was prepared to trade a sheep for a goat. Of course! An adventure! When I got to the Jeep it was full of automatic weapons. Hey, not this old Quaker. I said, "You call them on the phone and tell them you have a crazy American with you and you are coming unarmed." Dan then told me that he had killed a member of that family. But we talked and talked and he finally decided to do it my way. No, instead of being the enemy, we were guests in their home. They gave us the best they have, Near Eastern coffees. Now, to me, this is terrible stuff – strong, bitter coffee full of sugar to make it a kind of syrup. Sugar was very expensive for them. When my very small cup was finally gone, they offered more. I said, "Very good, but no thank you." Dan told me, "Get your coffee and don't make me trouble!" I was a good boy, they traded the sheep for the goats, and we went home happy. The distrust between these cultures has gotten so much worse since then, I don't know if it could happen today.

This final story is a high point in my life because it is so basic as an example of what we should be trying to do in this life.

Right after Khrushchev and Eisenhower agreed to cultural exchanges, I went to the Soviet Union. I was in one of the first groups to go over. You had to be in a group. Our group was terrible. They were uptight and drinking too much. I went to the government guide and said that this behavior was awful and asked if I could leave the group and just walk the streets and make friends. She told me to go ahead. I located a Baptist church and they were about to begin their services. I stood in the back, looked pathetic and spoke only English. They brought Reverend Orlov over to me, the Minister to Foreigners. He had gone to the seminary in England so his English was better than mine. He had spent time in detention under the Communist rule. It was going to be crowded. I said that I would like to worship with them and I would just stand in the back. He said, "No you won't." He took me up and seated me in the first row of the balcony.

Halfway through that service the entire congregation stood up and sang the Christian hymn, "Blessed Be the Ties that Bind." That says it all.

Case Studies and
Discussion Points

1. The case of the deal gone sour

I went to Germany to negotiate the purchase of a masonry-tool business. Their tools were better than ours and I wanted to acquire the technology. We negotiated a deal. Finally, I said, "Who should set the deal? If the other doesn't like it, we'll just shake hands and part company friends. But we won't haggle."

I figured that if he set the deal and he wanted to sell, he'd set the price low enough so he'd know that I'd buy it. But if I set the price and I wanted to buy, I'd set the price high enough so I'd think he'd sell.

We put the proposed terms down on a piece of legal-sized paper, which carried no legal weight. It was very informal. I initialed a corner of it, and he did likewise. When I got home, I got a call: A competitor, Black & Decker, had just raised the ante.

What do you do?

1. Renegotiate and sweeten the deal.
2. Consult counsel about initiating a lawsuit or entering into arbitration.
3. Or tell this guy to go shinny up a flagpole and rotate.

My first response was the correct one: I had done business with a nogoodnik. And that's a no-no. I have on occasion done business with a nogoodnik, and I've always paid for it. So I told the guy, "You've just done business with Black & Decker."

You don't get points for dealing with a smart donkey. It turns out that Black & Decker had endless troubles with this guy in Germany. They even had to take a write-down on their balance sheet. My feeling is, "Thank you, Black & Decker!" They did me a good turn.

NOTES:

2. The case of the mangled arm

At Universal Woods, we had a tragic accident. An employee got his arm caught in a machine. The arm was mangled and he was very badly hurt. We tested him for drugs, and it was positive. Drugs caused the accident. Drug testing is standard procedure at our company.

What do you do?

1. Get the man into counseling and give him another chance.
2. Give him a leave of absence.
3. Fire him.

We fired him outright.

Admittedly, it was cruel. Here was a guy that was put on the human scrap pile with no termination settlement of any kind. He had workmen's compensation, but that's all he had.

But his drug addiction could have resulted in a co-worker's death. We have a dangerous operation here, and we work hard to maintain good safety procedures. In fact, I sit on the safety committee. We have a good record.

But we had to let the employee go, and we had to do it in a way to send the message: Drug-use is just plain unacceptable. You must have a safe working environment for all employees.

NOTES:

3. The case of the buried tank

Vermont American sold a piece of property and the new owner discovered a gasoline tank buried there. We had not known about the tank, but it posed an environmental problem and had to be removed.

What do you do?

1. Call the lawyer quickly.
2. Tell the new owner to find the culprit and get him/her to clean it up.
3. Tell the guy to clean it up, and send us the bill.

We trusted the man who had bought this lot from us. Otherwise, we would have cleaned it up. But we ended up telling him to do that and send us the bill. Clearly, we should have known about the tank. We should have done an environmental audit of the property when we owned it.

Most of my students urge me to call the lawyer right away. My reply, "Lawyers are irrelevant" and my students get all upset – particular the lawyers in my class. But you don't need a lawyer. It's a simple matter – you've got to clean it up! Taking responsibility is the ethical thing to do.

NOTES:

4. The case for income tax payments

Vermont American employed a Swede who asked that his paycheck be sent to a New York bank and not Sweden.

What do you do?

1. Go along because tax payments are his responsibility, not ours.
2. Try to ensure that he's meeting his tax obligations.

I said, "Sure, I'll do it, as soon as you write me a letter saying you've paid your income taxes."

Later he thanked me. He would have faced the possibility of a fine and maybe prison for evading taxes. It turns out another company did in fact send a check to him in care of a New York bank, and he got caught with that one.

He called me and said, "I paid a big penalty. But if you had sent my check to New York like the other company did, that would have been a big enough problem that I would have ended up going to jail."

NOTES:

5. The case of commission or no commission

I had just been appointed CEO of Vermont American when I learned that we were paying the purchasing agent of a company a five-percent commission to act as our sales agent.

What do you do?

1. Forget it. There are more important things to worry about.
2. Cease the payments immediately. This is bribery.

This was a no-brainer. My immediate reaction was, "We've got to stop this nonsense." In India, they would call this baksheesh. In America we call it a bribe. You shouldn't pay baksheesh. I don't care where in the world you do it, baksheesh is baksheesh.

We stopped the payments and lost the account overnight— $100,000 on a $9 million business. We paid a heavy price for our ethical stand: We were forced to lay off four or five workers in the plant. That's too bad. Later we developed some business to replace the lost account and hired them back, but they were laid off for awhile.

NOTES:

6. The case of the closet homosexual

Vermont American ran a plant in a conservative community in the South. One of our employees was a closet homosexual. He was up for a promotion and transfer to another facility.

What do you do?

1. Keep him where he is and not rock the boat.
2. Promote him.
3. Do nothing and build a case for eventual discharge.

I try to know God's will for me, but I don't pretend to know God's will for you. If someone is a homosexual, that's his business. I don't care if he's in the closet or out of the closet. He's entitled to make his contribution to the company. And if he's ready for a promotion, he should be promoted. We shouldn't give a hoot about anything else.

We promoted him.

If he'd been open about his sexual orientation, we would have done the same thing and taken the heat for it.

NOTES:

7. The case of the unethical competitor

Vermont American had 60 percent of the power tool accessory business and a competitor had 60 percent of the power tool business. They came out with a promotion offering a percentage discount on both power tools and accessories if you'd buy the whole line from them. Clearly this was a violation of anti-trust laws.

What do you do?

1. Take them to court.
2. Don't take them to court.

Bob McDermott, a member of our board and an attorney, gave this advice, "If you take these people to court, you will have them and the government all over you trying to find evidence." Bob came to his conclusion based on practical grounds, the same as I came to my conclusion on ethical grounds.

Based on my religious principles, I'm against taking people to court. Besides, a lawsuit creates enemies and you should try to build partnerships, not make enemies. In this case, even the lawyer told me that going to court was a bad idea. He said that's because the government and our competitor would then be able to crawl all over us with discovery and a lawsuit wouldn't be worth our while.

NOTES:

8. The case of the imperfect invention

Vermont American created a super hard carbide tool that would outlast ordinary carbide in many applications. It was also more brittle and not suitable for fiberboard and particleboard— as a potential customer discovered during testing. (Ironically this was Universal Woods, the company I later purchased).

What would you do?

1. Inform the prospect of the tool's limitations.
2. Sing its praises and not disclose the downside.

We should have told them up front. That would have been the ethical thing to do. This prospect never did any business with Vermont American, and it's easy to understand why. They went through all of that testing, and the tool obviously wasn't suitable.

It all boils down to this: Tell the whole truth and nothing but the truth— even if it hurts your business.

NOTES:

9. The case of the chatty human resources director

The department director at Vermont American disclosed some confidential information about an employee.

What do you do?

1. Counsel with him and maybe seek professional help.
2. Fire him.

We fired him. The man proved he didn't have good ethical sense and you can't have people like that in your company. However, later we didn't try to keep him from getting another job. Hopefully he learned a valuable lesson. But he wasn't going to stay with our company to try to make amends.

NOTES:

10. The case of the nasty strike

In Virginia, a union shop is not legal, so you end up with non-union and union people working alongside each other. That creates a sort of built-in antagonism during a strike. Vermont American ran a plant in Bristol, Va., which was dedicated to a single customer, and the union went on strike. (Ironically, we had gotten the business because a previous supplier had a nasty strike and neglected the customer.)

What do you do?

1. Cave in and be non-competitive.
2. Insist all office people cross the picket line and work in the factory. (Virginia is a right-to-work state so not everybody must be in the union.)
3. Fire all strikers and hire all replacements.

We took option 2: To cross the picket line, to keep the plant open. Because violence was always a distinct possibility, I was the first guy across the picket line. If I crossed the picket line, I reasoned, there wouldn't be any violence. And there wasn't. A few homes of non-union people were spray-painted, but no individual was attacked.

We had guards walking the roof of the building. They were armed – but only with cameras. A union worker wouldn't dare take out a gun because then he'd be on Candid Camera!

The only physical violence was after the strike was settled. One of the key people crossing the picket line was a maintenance guy who kept the machinery running. Somebody stole his tools. He was sure it was the union president, and he hit the guy with a two-by-four.

Naturally, we couldn't tolerate that and we had to fire him. Under the circumstances, I felt badly for him and bought him a new set of tools out of my own pocket.

But in the long run we were never able to get rid of the antagonisms, the tension between strikers and no-strikers. They were never able to get along. So we ended up closing the plant. It's a tragedy.

Every time there was a strike in our company, I worked the factory line. After the strike was settled, I'd stand behind the guy who was doing the job I had been doing, and say, "I'll be damned, that's how you do it right, isn't it?"

The lesson I learned from that and other strikes at Vermont American is, what do you see when you look in the mirror? How does what you're doing look to the person looking at you? How does this deal you're about ready to make look to the other person? You've got to put yourself in the shoes of the other person.

NOTES:

11. The case of the basic buying contract

Sears was Vermont American's biggest customer. When a 600-pound gorilla suggests something, you listen. So when Sears proposed a basic buying contract, we had a selling job to do.

What do you do?

1. Negotiate a better profit percentage.
2. Agree, but restrict the deal to a single plant dedicated to Sears.
3. Tell them to go shinny up a flagpole and rotate.

A basic buying contract is cost plus. Sears auditors wanted to come in and oversee our operation. They wanted to help us reduce our costs so they would get their product cheaper. My question was, "So who's going to run this show? Are they going to run it or are we going to run it?" Well, I didn't want them running it. Or else why would they need me in the picture. Furthermore, under a basic buying contract you don't have the incentive you need.

We turned them down. We told them we didn't think it was a good idea at all. When we run our own show, we're going to do business with other people. We're going to build up volume. And our volumes are going to be built in such a way that we're going to build up economies of scale. We'll do better for you that way, we argued. We had already come down in price for Sears once at our own initiative. We needed to have a partnership arrangement, and in that way we'd make more money.

We sold Sears that a basic buying contract was a bad idea—and they bought our argument.

12. The case of the bad batch of screws

When I was a buyer for Vermont American, we were paying five cents for socket head cap screws from Rockford Screw Co. A new source quoted a price of four cents. I told Rockford that they were not competitive. They reduced their price allowing me to justify splitting the business. When the screws came in from the new source, they were trash and we rejected them. I placed their half of the order back with Rockford.

In dealing with Rockford, I should pay:

1. Four cents for all.
2. Five cents for all.
3. Half at the first price, and half at the second price.

I had haggled Rockford down based on false information. The other people couldn't make good screws. The only conclusion was that we've got to pay Rockford five cents each for the whole order.

They were very surprised, but what happened was not that surprising: We formed a partnership. We figured we could go to work to get the price down. But we did it as partners. We did it together.

NOTES:

13. The case of burn vs. bury

The surface of our products at Universal Woods must be smooth. You can't laminate on something that's rough. We use sanders in our operation, and we generate a lot of sawdust. How do you get rid of it?

You have two choices:
1. Burn it, but you end up putting the particulate in the air.
2. Bury it in a landfill.

Neither option is any good. We investigated other options, but came up empty-handed.

We send the waste to a landfill, where they use the sawdust as a liner. That's a little better than just dumping it on top of the landfill. It's not a perfect solution, but it's the lesser of two evils.

Otherwise, we go out of business. I don't like it one bit. But if you have no alternative, what are you going to do?

Sometimes you have a situation you don't like. We're making a product that's useful. If you buy decking material from one of our competitors, you will probably smell their plant a block away. They're not curing their sawdust before they burn it.

Except for the sawdust, our plant is green. We're curing everything. You can't smell this plant. We're more environmentally friendly than our competition, which is one of the reasons that I bought this place.

We try to run an ethical and environmentally responsible business. We're not perfect, as this case so amply proves. But we try as hard as we can, and that's what counts.

14. The case of the distributor who declined

We have developed a three-way partnership. Our resin supplier partner and we have jointly developed a static-resistant decking board for use in applications where static electricity is a problem for electronic equipment. Our distributor partner buys the board for resale. Our distributor declined to take an order from a manufacturer of fighter planes on ethical grounds.

What are the ethical issues?

NOTES:

15. The case of paying baksheesh...or not

Our Philippine sales agent was not performing satisfactorily. I found him to be conscientious and personable. He stated that he had two problems. First, he would not pay baksheesh, and second, most of the potential customers were ethnic Chinese. He suggested an ethnic Chinese agent that he thought could do the job on both counts.

Should we change agents? What are the ethical issues?

NOTES:

16. The case of racial prejudice

We hired an African-American sales manager around 1970. Immediately we lost the largest potential account in the territory. We had been getting a portion of that business and it was substantial. We proved that it was strictly a racial issue.

I should:
1. Tell the sales manager to do the best that he can and we would continue to work with him.
2. Reassign the sales manager to another job even though it would have to be less responsibility.
3. Help him to shinny up somebody else's flagpole.

We had an opening for an accountant at Universal Woods. There had never been an African-American in the office. There were several in the factory. There were two finalists. One could step right in and do the job. The other, an African-American, was a college graduate but would require some training. Can I take race into account in making this hire?

NOTES:

17. The case of the missing information

My brother-in-law and I were on the board of Thomas Industries when my father died. At that point, the management stopped giving us the information necessary to be conscientious board members. They thought we might cause the company to be sold to provide liquidity to the estate.

We could go to court and get the information. Should we? What are the ethical issues?

NOTES:

18. The case of the hospital donation

I have prostate cancer. If I have brachytherapy in Seattle the cure rate is 93%. Any place else it is 85%. I am on Medicare. The Seattle hospital will lose several thousand dollars if they accept me as a patient because of the amount Medicare will pay for this procedure, so they decline to accept me. It is illegal for me to make up the difference.

I make a substantial contribution to the charity fund at the Seattle hospital. Now they accept me as a patient. Did I do something unethical? Why or why not?

NOTES: